S0-BSN-907

A PIECE OF PARIS:
THE GRAND XIVTH

AN IDIOSYNCRATIC GUIDE TO AND HISTORY OF THE XIVth ARRONDISSEMENT IN PARIS

(Being a Portion of a Work in Progress on the City of Paris and its Fate)

by

Brewster Chamberlin

For Andrea,
with love and the memory
of Apt!
Brewster
8/8/96

Masurovsky Publishing Company
Washington, D.C.

This book was produced on a Macintosh Quadra in QuarkXpress and printed by Kirby Lithographic Company, Inc., in July 1996.
This first edition numbers five hundred copies, of which one hundred copies are numbered.

ISBN 0-9645937-0-X

Library of Congress
Catalog Card Number
96-077744

Copyright © 1996 by Brewster Chamberlin
All rights reserved

Drawings by Gregory Masurovsky
Copyright GM/S.P.A.D.E.M., Paris, 1995
All rights reserved

Photographs by Philippe Simon

First Edition
published by

Masurovsky Publishing Company

a division of

CyberTrans International, Inc.
1100 Connecticut Avenue, NW
Washington, DC 20036

For

Lynn-Marie Smith

this memorial

to her beloved city

with love

Preface

These notes on the 14th arrondissement of Paris are part of a larger work on the city which encompasses most of the other arrondissements and consists of recommendations, with appropriate descriptions and comments, to restaurants, cafés and hotels which may be of use to travellers to the French capital, sometimes referred to as The City of Light and, by certain Frenchmen, as The Cultural Capital of the World. As the notes below indicate, the larger work also contains much history and opinion about various people, events, and ideas which have and continue to interest me. It is, of course, my hope that these things will also be of interest to my readers, may they increase in numbers and wealth.

My friend, Marc Masurovsky, an American born and bred in Paris, the proprietor of the parent company of the publishing house which has published *A Piece of Paris: The Grand XIVth*, offered me the opportunity to have a section of the larger work in progress see the light of print before it is published as a whole. I am grateful to him for this chance to test the waters, so to speak.

Several matters, explained in the larger text, require a brief explanation here. The "we" refers to me and Lynn-Marie Smith, who shares my life and passion for Paris.

The avoidance in the text of the traditional descriptive usage in naming the events generally referred to as World War I and World War II, stems from my well-founded belief that they constitute, in fact, one event interrupted by a short inter-regnum of relative peace. The nomenclature I use to refer to this event may seem to some as rather affected, but a few moments' consideration should suffice to elicit the conviction that the phrases are perfectly accurate and justified.

i

Certain circles in France and elsewhere traditionally refer to the primitive toilet facilities, which consist of a hole in the ground and two somewhat elevated and occasionally slippery foot-pads, as a Turk. In the interest of brevity and pungency of narrative thrust, I have adopted this usage.

What may appear occasionally as an error of spelling or, more generously, as a misprint, should not be credited as such. Rather these usages reflect a deliberate intention to create a more succinct, reasonable, and aesthetically attractive printed page, in addition to indulging in various forms of wordplay in several instances. For all intensive purposes these are not mistakes, though some may consider them mistaken.

The following people have contributed in one form or another to the creation of the work in hand: Lydia Perry, who started it off several years ago when she innocently asked for Paris hotel and restaurant recommendations; Heidi J. Fleischer, who diligently manipulated the computer software to create a pleasing and sharp page layout; Aaron Kornblum, who provided research assistance; Margaret Corman, who provided those magnificent oysters and vin blanc, sustenance for the workers in the vineyards of nostalgia in her adopted city; Peggy Frankston, who introduced me to Philippe Simon, the photographer; Denis Constancias, who helped with the translations; and Benton Arnovitz, who provided much needed and much welcomed advice on how to deal with being published.

I owe a special debt of gratitude to Gregory Masurovsky, who created the illustrations, and who has shared with us so much of his Paris, where he has lived for 40 years.

Needless to say, none of these generous people are in any way responsible for errors of fact or my opinions in the text.

Washington DC, April 1996

Table of Contents

Photographs appear on pages 79-86.

Arbitrary geography be damned! Or at least ignored. The dyspeptic cartographers who blindthly drew a line down the length of the Boulevard du Montparnasse, dividing the 6th from the 14th arrondissement, could not have known the trouble they would cause writers writing about the quarter of the city emotionally centered at the intersection of that thoroughfare and the Boulevard Raspail. For some arcane reason, the cartographers named this crossroads the Carrefour Vavin. The contingent places in question here cannot be divided by arrondissement, or any other recondite mental construct; rather, we must represent them as they exist in an ambient non-geographic reality; that is, an area the boundaries of which have been determined by the protean ebb and flow of human society in its multifarious forms of rational and irrational intercourse. This is one case wherein a force other than mere geography and the bureaucracy's capriciousness must be the determinant, namely convenience and history. This is the quarter referred to generically as Montparnasse and known to the 1920s expatriate generation as "The Quarter," as they were known, amongst themselves and by their critics, as "The Quarterites."

✳✳✳✳

An overly nostalgic but still sentient littérateur might mildly complain that we do not write of certain places of importance, historically speaking, c'est-à-dire, such as the **Dingo Bar**, 10, rue Delambre, where F. Scott Fitzgerald and various personages who appear under different names in *The Sun Also Rises* gathered to drink themselves silly and merry, if possible at someone else's expense. In the interest of clarity, I should note that this is a guide mainly to places that are, not those which have been, although Lynn-Marie and I clearly are attached to a number of the latter, and they do tend to get mentioned, even during an explanation of why they might not be mentioned. The Dingo Bar was for years called L'Auberge du Centre, but is currently named L'Auberge de Venise, and we have not yet put our elbows on the bar there, which is alleged to be the same one that all the expatriates put their own sodden elbows on.

✳✳✳✳

We have, however, put our bottoms on the chairs in the **Restaurant Dominique**, at 19, rue Bréa (6th), the management of which extolls it as the oldest Russian restaurant in Paris, which may indeed be true, given that it opened in 1927. More importantly, the food is good depending upon the chef's mood, the wine list is more than adequate and the atmosphere is as friendly as the prices are relatively moderate. For those who care about such things, the place is not air-conditioned, a fact to be considered when choosing a restaurant without a terrace during a heat-wave. There is a bar of sorts, but more for eating than drinking in the American tradition. If no table in the restaurant proper is free, sit at the bar or at

2

The Auberge de Venise, formerly the Dingo Bar.

one of the tall round bar tables; the menu is quite similar.

In the summer of 1992, we ate dinner here with Pierre Capretz, a Yale professor who created the videotaped Annenberg/CPB Project *French in Action* language course, and Sylvie Mathé, a professor at the University of Aix-en-Provence. At one point the people at the table next to ours rose to leave and the American woman in the group leaned over and hoarsely whispered to Professor Capretz, "You do a great show!" and wafted out of the restaurant. To his credit, Professor Capretz did not know what she meant until we explained the vulgar phrase to him. The wine he chose that night fully supported the meal and, indeed, in my case, far outshone it in taste and satisfaction. Pierre Capretz certainly does a great wine choice.

If you turn to the left when leaving Dominique and turn left again at the intersection corner, you will find, once more on your left, the **Rue de la Grande Chaumière**. Walk into this brief street and linger for a moment, thinking of those who lived and studied here: Stephen Vincent Benét, Manuel Ortiz de Zarate, Paul Gauguin, Nathanael West (in the Hôtel Libéria at number 9 during the Winter of 1926-1927), Alphonse Mucha, Amedeo Modigliani and his unfortunate, but ethereal love Jeanne Hébuterne, Jules Pascin, Nina Hamnett, August Strindberg (at number 12 where he experimented in alchemy), and Rudolf Levy (who took over the direction of Henri Matisse's Académie when the painter found the students too exhausting), all lived in the street at some point. At number 10 you stand before the deservedly famous **Académie Colarossi**, where so many known and unknown artists taught and studied that a list of them would fill a hefty volume. In 1870, a former artists' model, Colarossi, took over the Académie Suisse, the oldest (1815) such institution in Paris, and moved it under his name to the Rue de la Grande Chaumière, where it prospered.

✳✳✳✳

But mull over in your mind the names Anna Diriks (wife of the Norwegian painter, Edvard), Helene Schjerfbeck, Jules Pascin, Kuroda Seiki, Jeanne Hébuterne, Thora Dardel, Antoine Bourdelle (teacher of sculpture, who must have suffered many jibes at his name), Robert W. Service, and Gauguin, who briefly taught there. And, then, the name **Krohg**: the free-spirited, not to say promiscuous Oda; her husband, Christian, paterfamilias and teacher at the Académie; and Per, the son who studied with his father at the Académie.

Per Krohg also studied at the Matisse Academy, where in the Spring of 1910, Cécile Vidil, known as Lucy, posed for the students. In the Autumn of 1910, Lucy and Jules Pascin engaged in a brief affair when she posed for him at his Montmartre studio. In December 1910 or January 1911, Lucy began to pose for Per in his studio at 9, rue Campagne-Première in Montparnasse. Legend has it that they fell in love at the Bal Bullier, an elaborate dance-hall formerly at 33, avenue de l'Observatoire across the intersection from the Closerie des Lilas. The story of the incredible inter-secting lives and loves of Per, Lucy and Jules and their friends who became lovers, wives, husbands, and friends again, would, alas, consume too much space here. The complex dance of their lives (at one point

5

during the First Chapter of the Great World Assininity, Per and Lucy became the tango king and queen of Scandinavia) continued on and off the dance-floor for more than twenty years with Paris as its main locus.

Billy Klüver and Julie Martin have printed in their misleadingly titled but indispensable book, *Kiki's Paris: Artists and Lovers 1900-1930* (1989), a photograph of the nude Lucy standing in the doorway of the Rue Campagne-Première studio in 1911 or 1912, her hair in a short bob she wore a decade before it became de rigueur, a turtle crawling slowly across the floor of the seemingly empty studio ... she stares with sad but unflinching eyes at the camera, at the observer-voyeur, as if she already saw the bloody end of Jules Pascin, who would write in a suicide note to her on June 2, 1930, "Lucy, don't blame me for what I am doing. Thank you for the packages. You are too good, I must leave so that you can be happy! Adieu! Adieu!" and who would scrawl on his door in his own blood "Adieu Lucy." But surely something else caused the sadness. Or perhaps it is not sadness at all, perhaps that is only what I see in this evocative, contradictory image of raw sensuality and preternatural knowledge then.

✳✳✳✳

At number 14, the **Académie de la Grande Chaumière** opened in 1906 and served as a school for Augusta Savage, William Gordon Huff, Berenice Abbott, Abraham Rattner (a sadly neglected American painter), Caresse Crosby (at least she claimed to have studied here), Alexander Calder (whose work may be cute but is on the whole overrated, like that of Matisse, whose work may not be cute but is certainly overrated), Anaïs

6

Nin, Isamu Noguchi, Pierre Matisse (yes, yes, it is his son), Alberto Giacometti (about whom his fellow students prophesized: "he will either go very far or go mad" and whom they called "the crazy genius" due to his solemnity and actual seriousness about being an artist and creating high art), the very talented and tragic Flora Lewis Mayo, Laura Wheeling Waring and hundreds of others. Some considered the Grande Chaumière better than the Colarossi, perhaps because Antoine Bourdelle and Fernand Léger occasionally taught there.

Bourdelle, who also taught at the Colarossi, querrelled with his student Giacometti; how could it have been otherwise given their diametrically opposed visions of what sculpture actually *is*. James Lord reports Bourdelle telling the young Alberto: "One can do things like that at home, but one doesn't show them." But where are Bourdelle's pieces today? If one looks hard and long enough one may find some, but Giacometti's are prominently displayed in the great museums of the world, especially prominently at the Fondation Maeght in Saint-Paul-de-Vence. Do I believe Alberto Giacometti to be one of the greatest sculptors of the 20th century? Woof!

The school is still open, should you, dear reader, wish to join the list of those who sat in the uncomfortable studios and gave their lives meaning, creating something eternal. (For me lists of names are not filler, but rather suffuse my mind with the radiance of the past in long rolling waves of nostalgia, a phenomenon which I would no doubt denigrate in others.)

7

If you come back out to the Boulevard du Montparnasse and turn to the right, you will walk past Rodin's statue of Balzac on the island in the middle of the Boulevard Raspail. Balzac, it should be noted, was not noted for hanging about Montparnasse, probably because, like Dickens and Zola, he spent his time writing reams of copy to pay the rent. Across the street you will see the **Café du Dôme**, at 108, boulevard du Montparnasse (14th).

This historic establishment is both a café and a restaurant, the latter being expensive, but worth at least one full lunch or dinner (for two with a good wine ca. $120) so you can enjoy the quiet plush of maroon velvet and shining polished gold-gilded newel-posts and railings, in addition to one of the most elegant set of restrooms and telephone booths anywhere. We ate the best fresh oysters ever here. In the café section on the street, glass-enclosed in cold weather, one can sit for a while over a cup of coffee and watch the people, always worthwhile in Paris.

Le Dôme is "famous" as a gathering place for the 1920s expatriates from the USA and Great Britain, and elsewhere, but the French literary set have also collected here from time to time. And somewhere, someone, probably a White Russian or at least a retrograde tzarist agent, says Ilya Ehrenburg spent some bolshevik roubles here after the Rotonde became too americanized for him in the early Twenties.

Ehrenburg allegedly composed the ditty:

>Read all about us and marvel!

which sums it up pretty nicely, though the original Russian probably scans better. (What if he wrote this doggerel in English?!)

One source tells us the Dôme is the oldest of the Montparnasse cafés (the word used loosely) starting out in 1897 as a laborers' saloon with a billiard table and no customers even pretending to high culture. The tale about the workers' bar, however, probably refers to the much smaller bar of the Rotonde across the street, which did begin as a standup coffee and marc drinkerie, although some memoirs note that coachmen and other laboring men stood at the Dôme bar enjoying an apératif and discussing whatever coachmen discuss at bars. Lenin, Trotsky and some of their revolutionary colleagues allegedly met in the Dôme on occasion before 1914 and photographs from the antebellum era show only a few tables and chairs in front of the establishment. Klüver and Martin's big book has the photographs and a text whose validity seems only occasionally to be in need of shoring up.

In fact, Klüver and Martin give the opening date as 1898, and 1902 as the date of the two billiard tables' installation in the backroom. It seems that a group of American painters from the schools and studios in the Rue de la Grande Chaumière and the surrounding neighborhood immediately acquired squatters' rights in the backroom by running a game of poker which lasted for a decade or more. However, one source says the Americans played billiards forever and the Germans' group played poker in the front rooms. Take your pick.

The results of the Franco-German Belligerency of 1870-71, in which the Germans soundly defeated the French in what may have been the last "gentlemen's war" in history, cut France out of the German tour schedule for many years. But by the turn of the century memories had dimmed somewhat and in 1903 Rudolf Levy moved to Paris from Munich where he had been one of the leaders of a loose grouping of German painters. He and Walter Bondy, a Hungarian painter who had studied in Munich, began meeting in the Dôme, thus establishing a Stammlokal in the café's front space. So, if we believe all the sources, we have the Americans in the backroom playing poker and/or billiards, the coachmen at the bar drinking coachman cocktails, the bourgeoisie on the banquettes with their apéritifs and newspapers, and the Germans at the tables in the front space playing poker and smoking cigars, with the terrace as the only common meeting ground. Even if reality did not exactly mirror this arrangement, it is pleasant to think it did.

Levy and Bondy did not make a secret of their happiness at finding the café, and soon artists such as Albert Weisgerber, Hans Purrmann, Wil Howard, Richard Goetz and Friedrich Ahlers-Hestermann, the art dealers, Wilhelm Uhde, Henri Bing and Alfred Flechtheim, and writers such as Erich Mühsam began to think of the Dôme as their second Parisian home, or at least as their living room, since their sleeping quarters usually did not include sufficient space or comfort for socializing in groups numbering more than two. By 1908, the Germans had absorbed a number of other nationalities all of whom spoke German: Eastern Europeans,

Scandinavians, artists from the Balkan states - collectively they became known as les Dômiers. The Germans called the café "the cathedral," logically enough, since "der Dom" in German means "cathedral." Flechtheim, who later opened an art gallery in Düsseldorf, on being asked by Christian Zervos which artist had the greatest impact on Germany in the 20th century, unhesitatingly replied "Schmeling, the boxer." Of course as an habitué of the Dôme before 1914, he was much younger and less brash.

One thing the German Cathedralites retained in common with their fellow countrymen across the Rhine: they did not generally welcome women to their tables; at least this is the legend that has come down the garden paths of time to us. They made an exception, however, for Hermine David, whose mother claimed she (Hermine, not her mother) had been sired by a Hapsburg prince during a brief visit to Paris, but the reason for the exception was surely the daughter's talent as a painter rather than her dubious paternity. Though on occasion they brought their wives or mistresses with them, rarely at the same time, Hermine David was the only female "regular." The fact that she became the lover of Jules Pascin, a male "regular," in addition to her talent and ability not to be bored when they spoke German all night, of which she understood not a word, also contributed to her exceptional status in this circle.

In any event, the Germans thus added themselves to the polyglot stew simmering and occasionally boiling over in Paris during the brief ante bellum period in the early 20th century. This milieu has often been described and narrated and analyzed by the talented and the untalented, the experts and the amateurs. Adolphe Basler published a book entitled *La peinture, religion nouvelle* in 1926, in which he describes some of the stew's ingredients: "...expressionists from Smolensk, who came much later [a reference to Chagall?], followed by the dadaists from Moldo-Valachia [definitely Tristan Tzara], the constructivists from Leningrad [Pevsner, Gabo], the neo-romantics from Baluchistan, who were all there, and not just to drink vermouth-cassis." That last sounds vaguely threatening, and occasional violence did punctuate the evenings at the Dôme - no longer, of course, now that the place is a highpriced restaurant.

The war, of course, changed everything. In August 1914, the Germans disappeared from Paris along with many Frenchmen and others, if for different reasons, as the Germans had vanished in 1870, and would vanish again, if for a much shorter period, in 1939. In June 1940, they returned to France and again occupied the tables at the Dôme, though for the most part these were different Germans entirely, and the study of high art did not constitute a fundamental part of the reason for their presence.

✳✳✳✳

Most dramatically a change at the Dôme occurred during the winter of 1922-23: by Spring, in time for the infestation by American and British carbon units (as tourists are known in certain circles), what had almost been a neighborhood local had become a café four times its previous size with rows of tables and chairs on the sidewalk. The Dôme immediately became chic and a must if one wished to be seen by other tourists or artistes. At this point, the Dôme symbolized the idea of the "roaring twenties in gay Paree."

Jo Davidson has left us a concise description of the Dôme during the period before the opening of the Great 20th Century Slaughterhouse in 1914. "At the Dôme, one was certain to meet artists, poets, derelicts and other kindred spirits. It was open till two in the morning and you could go there for girls, chess, poker, billiards or conversation." But do not look for derelicts or billiards or poker now; the Dôme has transcended its origins.

❊❊❊❊

If you can find a copy of **Elliot Paul**'s *The Mysterious Mickey Finn; or, Murder at the Café du Dôme: an International Mystery* (1939) or its sequel *Huggermugger at the Louvre* (1940), and if you read them, you will have something of the feel of the place, the time and the quarter, and afford yourself a few hours of amusement because they are very funny. Elliot Paul, an editor on the Paris edition of the *Chicago Tribune*, assisted Eugene Jolas, a city editor of the *Chicago Tribune*, in editing *transition*, a literary periodical published in Paris during the 1930s, perhaps the most well-known of such "little magazines," having printed many sections of Joyce's *Finnegans Wake*, then called "Work in Progress." Paul's active private life precluded his giving sufficient attention to his editorial duties, so in 1928 Robert Sage, also on the *Chicago Tribune* staff, became co-editor. You can read examples of the work the journal published in a volume entitled *In* transition: *A Paris Anthology* (1990), which apparently a book-packaging company in London put together; there is no editor listed, but the ubiquitous Noël Riley Fitch has written a brief historical introduction. You can see the spot where the Hôtel de la Gare des Invalides (now destroyed) housed *transition*'s editorial cubicle at 40, rue Fabet. The street runs along the western edge of the Esplanade des Invalides. The cramped room on the fourth floor had a magnificent view, but the plumbing equalled a Turk.

"Wacky" is not too extreme an adjective for life at the Paris *Chicago Tribune* and we are fortunate that Waverley Root, a constant critic of *transition*, wrote about his years as a reporter for the paper: *The Paris Edition. The Autobiography of Waverley Root 1927-1934* (1987).

Elliot Paul also wrote two books about the life on Rue de la Huchette (5th), where he lived for several years during the Thirties, called *The Last Time I Saw Paris* (1942), and *Springtime in Paris* (1950), a sequel taking up the story upon his return after the war. Do not confuse Elliot Paul's book with the horrid 1954 Hollywood movie called "The Last Time I Saw Paris," which is actually, very loosely, based on F. Scott Fitzgerald's story "Babylon Revisited"!

You might also read the short piece entitled "The Nineteen Twenties: An Interior" by Nathan Asch, taken from his unpublished novel, *Paris Was Home*. Asch describes a night at the Dôme in great detail, including the restrooms, which were extremely primitive compared to the present facilities; in point of fact, then a veritable Turk. Asch's story can be found in George Plimpton's compilation of pieces from *The Paris Review*, unsurprisingly entitled *The Paris Review Anthology* (1990). As long as you are reading about the Dôme, see if you can find the October 1925 issue of *American Mercury* in which Sinclair Lewis, the first American writer to win the Nobel Prize for Literature, tasted his revenge against the younger crowd of American expatriate would-be writers in Paris who had insulted him. According to the story, Lewis showed up at the Dôme not quite sober and feeling sorry for himself one night, believing himself, no doubt correctly, to be ignored by the herd of the "crowd." He began bragging about his sales and boasted that his writing was equal to that of Flaubert, at which point someone bellowed across the terrace "Sit down! You're nothing but a bestseller!" A few months later, in his article, Lewis singled out the Dôme as the headquarters of shallow, ignorant, drunk, untalented American jerkdom. A nasty, and to some extent certainly justifiable, diatribe, which still did not make him a more than mediocre but lucky craftsman.

Since 1945, the Dôme has become a superior, and expensive, restaurant. The red *Guide Michelin* awarded it a star for many years, but this marking has disappeared from the 1993 edition. Nonetheless, we recommend it highly, if you're flush, for lunch or dinner. Make a reservation. (Recently the management has opened a small room across the Rue Delambre from the Café du Dôme, called the Bistrot du Dôme, with a limited selection and somewhat lower prices. We have eaten a fine seafood meal there.)

One cold grey early morning in October 1991, we found the Dôme a supremely relaxing haven when, drooping from a seven-hour airplane trip, we gratefully sighed into the café chairs at 8 AM, hotel room far from ready at this hour, to read the papers, drink nourishing and warming bowls of café-au-lait and taste the ineffable flavor of freshly baked flaky croissants. A fine way to return to Paris, exhausted but happy and in one's own quarter again. Of course, there are far less expensive cafés in the neighborhood where one can read the papers and drink coffee, if one wishes.

✳✳✳✳

The late, lamented, English-language Paris monthly called *Passion* publicly stated that **Le Select** (6th), obliquely across the street from the Dôme, serves the best croque-monsieur in Paris; we can substantiate the richness of the cheese and recommend one drink copious quantities of Kronenbourg beer to help digest this masterpiece of fast, if heavy, food. Otherwise, the café-bistro has long served as a gathering place for literary and artist types of various nationalities, especially Americans in the 1920s. Be reminded again that prices in such well-known places tend to be rather higher than similar cafés with no reputation located on side streets.

✳✳✳✳

A few doors down the Boulevard du Montparnasse from the Select and directly across the street from the Dôme, sits the equally well-known (and for the same reasons) **La Rotonde** (6th), which doesn't enjoy the croque-monsieur recommendation, but is similar to the Select except that the Rotonde inside is more of a traditional restaurant. We have not eaten there, but have lolled about the outside tables for an apéritif or a nightcap on various occasions. The Rotonde you drink and eat in today is not the Rotonde of literary and art history of an earlier 20th century epoch. Opened in 1911 at 105, boulevard du Montparnasse, the owners took over the Café du Parnasse at 103 in 1924 and doubled the size of the place. In the Summer of 1959, a developer razed the old Café Rotonde and plunked down the Rotonde Cinéma in its place. In the early 1960s the movie house showed foreign films of quality with earphones for French translations and permitted cigarette smoking. You can imagine an entire theater filled with Gauloise smoke and thin, intense, young French intellectuals of all six sexes seeking subtextual meaning in Howard Hawks' westerns. Now the rather small house shows the same current movies you can see anywhere else in the city. The "new" Rotonde is two doors down on the Boulevard Raspail corner across from Balzac's penetrating stare.

✻✻✻✻

One should, perhaps, at least mention, **La Coupole** (14th), a few doors down from the Dôme, across the street from the Select and the Rotonde, which forms the fourth of the quartet of café-restaurants situated in the Montparnasse-Raspail (Vavin) neighborhood, all of which appear in all the memoirs and biographies of all the creative (and some not so) people who have moved through the milieux d'art in Paris.

Opened with great brouhaha in December 1927, the place swiftly became one of the chic spots to be in, whether to eat, drink or be seen. Judging by the photographs of it in the 1930s the neon signs illuminated the Paris night as the drinks and the atmosphere lit up the customers.

Noël Riley Fitch, in her recent biography of Anaïs Nin's erotic life, notes that Lawrence Durrell, Henry Miller and Nin dubbed themselves the "Three Musketeers of La Coupole" during the late Thirties. One would love to have witnessed *those* shenanigans! Unfortunately, all most people are concerned about knowing these days relates to sexual peccadillos, the more obsessively perverse the better, not what Sonny Rollins once called "real matters."

In his curious biographical book about Sartre, John Gerassi calls La Coupole "an amazing institution....it was a restaurant mostly for exhibitionists and voyeurs." Be that as it may, Gerassi's subject and Simone de Beauvoir apparently ate quite often on the right "aristocratic" side, where the staff kept the masses at bay, so to speak. Indeed, Gerassi has a wonderfully apropos story of a lunch with Sartre and Herbert Marcuse during the latter's halcyon days as guru to the rebellious youth of the late 1960s. Since Sartre had never read anything by Marcuse, he asked Gerassi to come along to help him out. As Gerassi tells it, the lunch at La Coupole, of course, did not require such intervention because Sartre played Marcuse so well the latter thought the former possessed a thorough grounding in his works. Two aging gurus, with attendant, at La Coupole eating cassoulet, the plat du jour on Thursdays, diligently cleaning their plates and feeding their egos.

A few years ago, the owners completely renovated the inside and, according to those who know best, ruined a historic monument, the only one of the four in which one could dance to a real dance band. We've looked in the windows from time to time, but have thus far not ventured inside, which appears to be a great well-lighted barn or a railroad station waiting room with tables. For a vicarious look at what it may have been like before the barbarians got their grubby paws on it, see Françoise Planiol, *La Coupole: 60 ans de Montparnasse* (1986), which quotes our friend Gregory Masurovsky frequently, but misspells his name.

Mr. Masurovsky, who has lived and worked not far from the carrefour Vavin since the mid-1950s, has written (1991) a short, informal explanation of the "new Coupole."

> René Lafon, the original owner, *sold* the Coupole
> to a Monsieur Bucher who directs the restaurant
> group "Flo," a group of brasseries in Paris
> characterized by their often "authentic" turn-of-the-
> century type décor, real or renovated. They are in the
> middle to lower-high price range (around 200 francs
> per person, I would venture).

> When Mr. Bucher bought La Coupole, he had it gutted
> so the present office building could be built on the site.
> He reproduced "his Coupole" afterwards, which has
> little in common with the original, but the cooking is
> good. It's just that the ambiance and the life-style
> that made for the charm of the place has been
> eradicated. One ought to call it, as someone mentioned,
> "La Coupole II." It is very successful and very noisy.

Clearly, we are not the only people who suffer depression when thinking about unnecessary and detrimental change. The famous phrase "plus ça change, plus c'est la même chose" does not apply to the wanton destruc-

The huge restaurant sits across the boulevard from the Select and down
the boulevard from the Dôme.

tion of cultural artifacts, the process of which also transgresses the ancient proverb, "If it aint broke, don't fix it."

Someone says somewhere in someone's obiter dicta that French intellectuals moved from the cafés at the Carrefour Vavin to those in St-Germain des Prés in 1940 after the Germans occupied the Dôme and its neighbors allegedly bringing their own coffee with them - insult to injury - but which is not surprising since they confiscated everything tasty or useful and left the French to drink a hot liquid made from chestnuts and tree bark. Nowadays, the Germans are indistinguishable from other European tourists in Paris and the coffee is both real and delicious, and you can sit for an hour for the price of one cup without waiter-pressure to order more or leave.

✳✳✳✳

If you travel south, either by métro or by foot, down the Boulevard Raspail, then right on Avenue du Général Leclerc, to the métro station Alésia, you will find it worth your culinary while to make a sharp turnabout, walk a block up Avenue du Maine, turn left into Rue du Moulin Vert and walk a further block until you reach Rue des Plantes. There, on the corner, at 34 bis, rue des Plantes, you will see the **Restaurant Au Moulin Vert**. During clement weather sit on the Terrasse d'Été. In the summer of 1992, when Gregory Masurovsky and Grethe Knudsen led us to this jewel, the prix-fixe menu was FF 170 per person, but included a bottle of good vin de table per couple! The food is of an excellent quality. This out of the way discovery could easily become our favorite Paris restaurant and we will certainly return on our next visit. (I wrote the last

21

sentence prior to our revisiting the place in October 1993, during which visit an overworked waitress spilled Gregory's rouget down his back. This can happen anywhere, well, almost anywhere, and most of the food ended on the floor, not on his shirt. The replaced fish tasted just fine, according to Gregory, and we all ragged the poor girl from the Auvergne a bit, but no one on the staff offered for the restaurant to pay the cleaning bill. This is not professional behavior for a restaurant of this caliber. On the other hand, the price increase over the previous year on the prix-fixe menu was only five francs and the food was delicious. And yes, we will still go back to eat there, but I can't speak for Gregory.)

One almost always appreciates imagination in a cook, as one appreciates attentive service and reasonable prices in a relatively quiet atmosphere. Gregory and Grethe introduced us recently to an exemplar of this rare phenomenon. **Les Petites Sorcières** can be found at 12, rue Liancourt, not far from the Denfert-Rochereau métro station. Although it could be described as a neighborhood restaurant, it is both popular and of limited seating, so a reservation is recommended (Tel.: 43 21 95 68). We found the unusual combining of traditional elements to be very tasty, although not to everyone's taste, so to speak. Melon with canard fumé and sauce béarnaise with veal kidneys worked wonderfully, but the chopped lamb and veg in phylo dough did not quite achieve the same level of success. We will definitely return here.

✳✳✳✳

The **Closerie des Lilas** (6th), several blocks down the street from the Dôme and the Select, at the corner of Boulevard du Montparnasse and Rue Nôtre-Dame-des-Champs, is another former tavern which is now a good, but very expensive restaurant. Curiously, the red Michelin doesn't mention it. Sit in the garden and have a drink, observe the statue of Marshal Michel Ney, sword raised as if to ward off the demons that may harm you, (the sword did not help him when the restorers of the Bourbons executed him on this very spot, on December 7, 1815, for supporting the return of Napoléon and command-ing troops at Waterloo), and contemplate the long literary history of the place. Ah, but things were cheaper then. The section in *A Moveable Feast* is apparently accurate on the Closerie for the early 1920s and brings vividly to life how the author remembers his youth in the city where he matured as a writer if not as a human being.

Keep in mind, however, that the Closerie Hemingway described disap-peared to a disheartening extent in the modernization the owner under-took in December 1925. If a waiter there tells you he remembers Monsieur 'Emingway, as one did to some naive tourists one night whilst we drank an apéritif, he's lying. If he tells you there is a name plate in the bar marking the very spot where Monsieur 'Emingway drank, he is, alas, not lying. Name plates also mark some of the very tables and places at the bar where some of the famous cultural figures of by-gone eras sat. Wow.

The Restaurant Au Moulin Vert; where excellent food and wine can be had for reasonable prices and where the unexpected occasionally happens.

According to some sources, the 1922 split in the modernist movement between the dadaists, on the one side, and others less tolerant of the purist puritanism of dada, on the other side, that led to the formation of the surrealist movement under the captainship of André Breton occurred at a meeting (a "gathering" might be more accurate, hardly the "congress" some of the participants thought it to be) in the Closerie.

Shortly before the "modernization" in 1925, the Closerie witnessed what may have been the last of the big banquets for literary figures organized by colleagues rather than agents or publishers with profits in mind. The poet thus honored no one, alas, remembers today: Pol Roux, known as Saint-Pol-Roux-le-Magnifique, according to Michel Leiris, one of the most brilliant, and last members of the symbolist generation. However, the occasion brought out the worst (or the best) in André Breton, whom the organizers should have known better than to invite. Thinking his friend Max Ernst had been insulted by an anti-German remark made by one of the speakers, Breton protested in such a manner as to provoke a melée of food-throwing, chair-hurling, fist-punching, oath-tossing, and insult-thrashing in which his fellow surrealist, Philippe Soupault, careened about hanging from a chandelier kicking everything animate and inanimate in his arced path. The sight of France's cultural figures, avant-garde or not, being led away in the panier à salade (Black Maria) and ambulances amazed the fascinated bourgeois pedestrians. Interestingly, years later Breton excommunicated Ernst from the Church of Surrealism because he refused to renounce his deep and lasting friendship with the poet Paul Eluard, previously excommunicated, and because he had the temerity to accept a prize for painting at the Venice Biennale.

****

The ubiquitous 'Emingway (at number 113, original building torn down and replaced), Ezra Pound (at 70 bis) and innumerable French people lived on **La Rue Nôtre-Dame-des-Champs**, conveniently around the corner from the Closerie. The strange poet and opium eater, Ralph Cheever Dunning, lived in a tiny room at 70 from 1905 until he died of exhaustion and debilitation in 1930. Hemingway wrote that Dunning forgot to eat and wrote poems in terza riruce when smoking opium and drinking liters of milk. Alice Toklas (before she moved in with Gertrude Stein in 1910) at 75, Ford Madox Ford at 84, Fernand Léger at 86, the sculptress Malvina Hoffman at 72, John Singer Sargent at 73 bis, Augustus St. Gaudens at 49, James McNeill Whistler at 86, and briefly Robert McAlmon at 59, also lived at various times in the Rue Nôtre-Dame-des-Champs.

From 1934 to 1936 Katherine Anne Porter lived in the Pounds' former apartment. Ten years earlier, when the Pounds moved to Rapallo, Italy, Janet Scudder moved into their flat. The once-famous American Impressionist, Alexander Harrison, lived for a while after 1888 in the building, as did Jean-Léon Gérôme (in 1861) and F. U. Wrangel (1888-89) when he wasn't gambling in Monte-Carlo. The now almost forgotten American cross-dressing painter, one of the few who learned the lessons of cubism, Morgan Russell, began his career in 1908 in a small studio on this street. Russell would remain in France through both parts of The

Great World Misery, returning to the USA only in 1946 to die near Philadelphia in 1953.

Rudolph Klément, born in Hamburg in 1910, worked for a number of years during the 1930s as Trotsky's secretary, until his arrest for driving without sufficient headlight illumination led to his employer's deportation from France in June 1935. Klément remained in Paris in fear and in hiding: NKVD assassins moved about the hemispheres at Stalin's behest conducting liquidations of Trotsky's followers. Klément hid in a small room in the Rue Nôtre-Dame-des-Champs and in another in the Passage de Vanves (where Léo Malet, the mystery writer, protected him) until August 1938 when the police fished his headless corpse out of the Seine. No one knows for sure who murdered Klément, but the presence of "Jacques Mornard" in the city at that time leads to certain conclusions, especially since three years later, under the name "Ramon Mercader," he appeared in Mexico City with an icepick in his luggage and eeled his way into the Trotsky household. Before too long he found the opportunity to crash the icepick into the exiled Russian's skull, thus completing his mission for his NKVD masters and ridding Stalin of his last real competition for the leadership of the communist world.

Well.

Just walking hurriedly through this street with another destination in mind will not do if one is to appreciate the thoroughfare's thick history. A list of those painters, sculptors and writers who lived and worked in this street's ateliers and apartments over several generations is astound-

27

ing in its length. For example, in addition to those already mentioned above: Camille Claudel; George du Maurier (dilettante); Émile-Auguste Carolus-Duran; Rosa Bonheur (partial source of Marcel Duchamps' cross-dressed nom de peintre "Rrose Sélavy"?); Augustin-Jean Moreau-Vauthier; Jean-Léon Gérome and his oddly trained monkey, Jacques; Jules Breton; Jean-Paul Laurens; François Bonvin; Henri Chapu; English sculptors Frederick William Pomeroy and Sir George Frampton; William-Adolphe Bouguereau whose giant genre paintings of Greek and Roman mythology scenes sold in the mid-19th century for so much money that he allegedly remarked, "I lose five francs every time I piss"; Charles Cottet; Manès Sperber; Henri Le Fanconnier, but why go on? The point is made.

Look up at the buildings. Notice, for instance, the cute little stone-mullioned doorway built into the glass façade of the top floor studio at 57-59, or the façade at 86 where Whistler kept his studio, or the more mundane present construction at 113 and 73 bis. For further details about the street's past, see John Milner's "lavishly illustrated" *The Studios of Paris* (1988).

✳✳✳✳

Victor Hugo lived at 11 during the years 1827-1830, where he sired the unfortunate Adèle and her brother François, and wrote his plays *Hernani* and *Marion de Lorme*. In his apartment, Hugo held open-house for fellow militant Romantics, including Balzac, Alexandre Dumas, Prosper Mérimée, Sainte-Beuve (who moved with his mother into number 19 in 1828 and began his relationship with Hugo's wife, also named Adèle),

Gérard de Nerval, Theophile Gautier, and Alfred de Vigny, and here they planned **The Famous *Hernani* Battle**. Indeed, after the premiere of the play and the tremendous scandal it caused, the owner of the building cancelled Hugo's lease in March 1830, forcing him to move his family to the Rue Jean-Gonjon.

Of what, some may justifiably wonder, does the "famous *Hernani* battle" consist, and why should one know anything about it? One could read about it at some length in Malcolm Easton's handy little volume, *Artists and Writers in Paris* (1964), or in any biography of Hugo. However, the jist of the matter is that Hugo wrote his play as a deliberate provocation to the predominant school of art and literature of the Bourbon restoration period, namely Classicism. Hugo and a group of fellow Romantics, the other end of the polarity (think of it as The Old Apollonian-Dionysian Duality), mounted an uproarious public relations program to ensure the succès de scandale they desired in what they viewed as the decisive battle with the previous generations' rigid and restrictive artistic methods, styles and subject matter, and the current State censorship of the written word.

According to plan, they turned the opening night, February 25, 1830, into a circus. Groups of young Romantics and Art Students converged on the Comédie-Française at mid-afternoon, armed with food and drink, and locked themselves in the theater for four hours during which time they ate and drank with abandon and giggles, one would like to think. Actually, the intensity of their youthful commitment to the cause probably precluded any real enjoyment of the event: no doubt they remained stoically sober. The respectable theater-goers who arrived at seven o'clock for the performance reeled with shock at the sight of the theater as a public restaurant. Garlic sausages and red wine, indeed! As the play went on, it became clear that the actors did not agree with its revolutionary message and scuffles between antagonists in the audience broke out throughout the performance.

And what an audience! Hugo's fan club dressed in outlandish costumes (scarlet satin waistcoats, 16th century Venetian doge outfits, oddly formed mustaches and beards, shoulder-length hair, and so on) rubbed and joggled elbows with the conservatively clad haute-bourgeoisie and residual aristocracy. The play ran for 45 performances and the Romantics considered themselves victorious.

No, Gérard de Nerval did not walk his lobster on a rhinestone leash down the theater aisle on this occasion. He accomplished that later on a fashionable Parisian thoroughfare. At the end of the 20th century, one finds it difficult to determine the "revolutionary" nature of the play's plot. In any case, Verdi's *Ernani* (1844) is based on Hugo's drama.

Robert W. Chambers lived in Paris from 1886 to 1893, and wrote hundreds of pages in books and short stories about the environs of the Left Bank. In one story, entitled "The Street of Our Lady of the Fields," he describes the Rue Nôtre-Dame-des-Champs thusly: "It is a pariah among streets - a street without a Quarter. It is generally understood to lie outside the pale of aristocratic Avenue de l'Observatoire. The students of the Montparnasse Quarter consider it swell and will have none of it. The Latin Quarter, from the Luxembourg, its northern frontier, sneers at its respectability and regards with disfavor the correctly costumed students who haunt it." Clearly a man writing before knowledge had unskinned his eyes and comprehension illuminated his brain. The street has been many things, but a pariah has never been one of them.

L'Entr'acte: Camille Claudel Chronology

1864   born Villeneuve-sur-Fère (Aisne).

1881   age 17, moves to Paris with mother and siblings, the latter to 135, boulevard du Montparnasse, Claudel to 117, rue Nôtre-Dame-des-Champs into an apartment with several English girls, begins study at the Académie Colarossi at 10, rue de la Grande Chaumière.

1885   meets Auguste Rodin, sculptor.

1888   Rodin rents work space for her, where she lives as well, in a building called La Folie Neubourg, a ruin of an 18th century villa at 68, boulevard d'Italie, allegedly so they could "work" together, actually to make it easier for him to steal her work and plunder her sexually as well, away from the watchful eye of his regular companion, whom he would marry in the end.

1892   breaks away, but not too far, from Rodin's manipulation, rents work space down the street at 113, boulevard d'Italie.

1899   moves to her final workspace, 19, quai de Bourbon on the Ile St-Louis, by which time her mind has begun to crack.

1913   interred in a mental institution as suffering from "dementia"; transferred at end of August 1914 to Montdevergues asylum in Montfavet near Avignon where, thanks to her brother Paul's indifference, she remains until

The Observatoire de Paris

1943 when, at the age of 79, she dies, after 30 years' incarceration. She is buried in the anonymous public Montfavet cemetery reserved for inmates of the asylum.

Adrienne Monnier sent Paul Claudel, then Ambassador in Washington, a free copy of the French version of *Ulysses* which she published in 1929. He returned the book to her declaring "I once wasted a few hours reading *Portrait of the Artist as a Young Man* by the same author, and that was enough for me....[Both books are] full of the filthiest blasphemies, in which one feels all the hatred of a renegade - afflicted, moreover, by a really diabolical absence of talent." This about a book in which even the most despicable characters are portrayed with a certain love and tenderness. No wonder he never understood his sister.

It is interesting that after the end of their relationship (ca. 1885), Rodin created no new sculpture and devoted himself to reproductions of his best pieces done while they worked together. Rodin, *the* modern sculptor, thief and wretch, brilliant and genius. O yes.

See the darkly wrenching, somewhat overwrought film entitled *Camille Claudel* (1990) for a passionate reenactment of their years together, with the perfect Isabelle Adjani as Claudel and the ubiquitous Gérard Depardieu as Rodin, the artistically gifted brute.

Fin de l'Entr'acte

Back on the Boulevard du Montparnasse, between the Rotonde and the Closerie there is a second-hand bookstore you should not pass by without going through the volumes on the sidewalk tables. We've discovered some nice bargains here, but one must be willing to spend the time to look closely. A selection of English language books is usually available, often in prewar Continental editions at very reasonable prices. Since a number of bookstores matching this description have sprouted in this stretch of the boulevard, you might wish to note that the one in question here is called **Les Nourritures Terrestres** and the address is 129, boulevard du Montparnasse.

✻✻✻✻

If you have created an appetite with all that browsing, you might try one of the restaurants along the same block as the bookstore. We've been to two of them in the Autumn of 1994, and one or both may appeal to you, depending on your tastes and mood. If you like a boisterous brasserie atmosphere in which you rub thighs with your neighbor whether you know him or her or not, but where the waiters are efficient and where you are served a good solid hot lunch (order the plat du jour), try the branch of the **Batifol** chain at 127, boulevard du Montparnasse, a door away from the bookstore. (This is a very busy place, so call for reservations: 43 20 63 02.) From 1925 to 1927, the building's ground floor contained the Monaco American Bar, about which little is known, and from 1927 until the early 1930s a night-club called The Jungle, which catered to American tourists and some of the less discriminating writers and painters, watered its drinks to make money from the tourists and the slumming bourgeois women who came late in the evening for the sweaty thrill of rubbing their bodies rhythmically against another person to the cacophonous blare of the thundering herd of an orchestra imported from some Carpathian village. As André Thirion described it during his own musical rubadubdub nights there: "extreme tensions of love and desire ... achieved by the tune 'I Can't Give You Anything but Love'." Henri, the former manager of The Jockey across the Boulevard, owned it and Hilaire Hiler, who designed the decor of The Jockey, created the decor here as well.

****

If, on the other hand, you require an eatery with a bit more class and less noise, and assuming you do not deny yourself seafood, try **La Langousterie** at 145, boulevard du Montparnasse. The glassed-in veranda contains an abnormal number of potted plants, but the food is good, well-prepared and served, and you don't have to spend the same amount we did to enjoy yourself, as the gentleman sitting to our left proved. On the other hand, we do like our wine and langoustes, and what the hell, we are only there for such short visits. Yes, well. (Telephone 43 26 63 39 for reservations.)

****

If you walk south on the Boulevard Raspail from the Carrefour Vavin, the second street you will see on your left is the **Rue Campagne-Première,** which, while not so permeated with European cultural history as the Rue Nôtre-Dame-des-Champs, is nonetheless studded with gems of past social and cultural glories if one has the imagination and time to call them up out of that vast storage bin we call history. On your right, as you walk up the street toward the Boulevard du Montparnasse, you will see the venerable Hôtel Istria at number 29 (double rooms cost between 465 FF and 570 FF in October 1994, but we've not stayed there). The façade has recently been renovated so it does not appear to be venerable, and if one's notion of venerable dates things from the 18th century then the place is indeed not venerable, but if one can accept as venerable a building with a history and importance dating from the year 1919, then the Hôtel Istria is venerable. Indeed.

A plaque on the hotel façade will tell you about its and the street's place in Parisian cultural history by simply listing the names of some of those who lived and worked on the street, a list which includes Man Ray, Rainer Maria Rilke, Louis Aragon, Elsa Triolet, Kiki, Francis Picabia, Marcel Duchamp, Moïse Kisling, Erik Satie, Tristan Tzara, and Vladimir Mayakovsky. The remainder of the plaque is taken up with a fragment from a poem entitled "Il ne m'est Paris que d'Elsa" by Aragon, the Stalinist poet and French Communist Party cultural functionary, whose self-degradation before the Party's quicksilver policy changes was so base and servile that one might perversely see it as almost heroic.

> Ne s'éteint que ce qui brilla ...
> lorsque tu descendais de l'hôtel Istria,
> tout était différent rue Campagne-Première,
> en mil neuf cent vingt neuf, vers l'heure de midi ...
>
> [Vanishes what once shone ...
> when you came out of the Istria Hotel,

everything changed on Rue Campagne-Première,
in nineteen hundred twenty-nine, around noon time...]

Indeed, Aragon and his life companion, Triolet, who also danced to the erratic rhythms of the Party's shifting music, lived next to the hotel at number 31 in 1929. Of course, nothing is as simple as that; although it is the truth, it is only a part of a larger truth, an exploration of which would offer a context for understanding their abject and deplorable behavior. Hélas, this is not yet the place for such an investigation. We have, as it were, other fishes of various sizes to fry here.

But we are not quite finished with the Hôtel Istria. The wall plaque does not tell you that Duchamp moved into the hotel in December 1923, most probably not with Thérèse Treize, as Arlen Hansen has it; she was a well-known model, teacher of gymnastics, and companion of painters at the time, whose name should have its place in a public site. Robert McAlmon lived here during the summer of 1927 and found a room in the hotel for William Carlos Williams, the poet and physician, and his wife, Flossie, when they sorely needed a place to stay during that summer of the American Legion 10th Anniversary, which during those months raged like the plague, infesting most of the hotel rooms in the city and country-side alike.

In 1922, that clever elf, the Surrealist painter and photographer Man Ray, rented a studio at number 31-31bis, having outgrown his earlier studio-apartment after shifting his creative emphasis on painting to photography, though he always considered himself foremost a painter, a painful irony for him given his world-reknown as a photographer. The double numbers reflect the fact that the building has two entrances. This unusual building (its façade stands out quite impressively from the rather more traditional façades on the street), constructed in 1911, contained not just studios, but living space as well. Man Ray's quarters stood just to the left of the 31 bis entrance on the ground floor. A narrow staircase at the back of the studio led to a 10 by 29-foot loft containing a toilet and sink, which Ray and Kiki used as a bedroom. If you really want to know, the studio measured 15 by 25 feet. Man Ray sent a postal card with a photograph of the street and the building to his parents in July 1922 noting "Here's where I live, $25 a month - a swell place!".

In 1923, Man Ray hired Berenice Abbott as his assistant, saving her from "mourant de faim," and she began here her apprenticeship as a photographer. Three years later, she began an independent and highly successful career with her own studio. In December 1923, Man Ray could afford to move into the Istria, and a number of sources say he did so at this time. One assumes Kiki moved in with him, at least at one point she had her own room there. (In the late 1920s, Man Ray rented a small studio at 8, rue du Val-de-Grâce in the 5th arrondissement in order to paint undisturbed. He maintained this studio at 31bis, rue Campagne-Première until 1937, when he moved into a combined studio and living quarters at 40, rue Denfert-Rochereau [now Rue Henri-Barbusse], where he lived until he left France in July 1940. Henri Hayden [1913-14] and Thérèse Treize [c. 1925-1930] also lived at the Rue Denfert-

Rochereau address.)

As you look at the Istria building, think about the following: in the Autumn of 1924, Francis Picabia and Erik Satie struggled there to create the ballet *Relâche*. Picabia also wrote the scenario for the short film, *Entr'acte*, which René Clair directed to be shown during the ballet's intermission following its premiere on December 4. Picabia, Satie, Man Ray and Marcel Duchamp all appear in the film; all four of them lived at the time in the Istria. A furious fount of fecundity, that hotel.

Continue on up the Rue Campagne-Première until you come to 17bis. Here in a bare apartment on the fifth floor from 1899 until his death in 1927 lived the photographer Eugène Atget and his life companion, Valentine Delafosse Compagnon. Once practically unknown and during the later years of his life poverty-stricken, Atget is now "world-famous" and requires no further description here. However, it should be recalled that, in a heroic gesture of cultural prescience, Berenice Abbott saved Atget's glass-plate negatives from the garbage pail after he died, and thus committed an altruistic act that allowed the old man's work to later become "world-famous" and the subject of many exhibitions and large-format books. Atget's photographs are quiet, filled with beauty (which often denies the squalid reality of the cityscape he is photographing), and should be known to anyone who has pretensions to being kulturny.

The next number (17) on that side of the street is an alley, with studios on both sides, which may always have been an alley, but which could have been a building at some past time. Mina Loy and her two lovely daughters, one of whom married the art dealer Julien Levy, Modigliani, Whistler, Rainer Maria Rilke, Mathilde Vollmöller, Malvina Hoffman, Stanley Hayter all lived and worked in this building. Hansen has Loy, as well as the Irish poet James Stephens, living at number 11, and Brian Morton's book on Americans in Paris has Loy at number 15, but number 17 is probably the correct address.

Number 9 is a building on a courtyard containing studios of varying sizes, mostly small to judge by the façades, built from metal and wood from the demolition of the 1889 World Exposition. Per and Lucy Krohg, Martin Kaelin, Walter Pach, and Léopold Gottlieb had studios there.

Further up the street at number 3 is the site of the well-loved eatery called Chez Rosalie, after its owner, cook and mother-hen to impecunious artists, models, laborers, and writers who frequented the place during its halcyon days 1906-1926.

Turn right on the Boulevard du Montparnasse, stroll for a block and turn right into the Rue Boissonade, which runs parallel to the Rue Campagne-Première. Elie Nadelmann, an East European sculptor lived at number 15 (1912-1914), as did the American sculptor, Mariette Mills (1920s); Amédée Ozenfant, the "cubist" painter and lover of Germaine Bongard, Paul Poiret's sister and art dealer, lived at number 16 (1911); Conrad Kickert, the Netherlandish painter (1925-1926), Edvard and Anna Diriks (1903-1923), painters from Norway and Sweden respectively; and Stella Bowen, for many years Ford Madox Ford's companion and mother of his daughter, Julia (1927- ?), all lived and worked at number 18. On the left as you look toward the building at number 19, gaze over the wall into a lovely park-like garden and wonder at the price of the apartments with such a view in the middle of the city. Then look up at number 19, and see if this art deco façade, from a certain angle, doesn't remind you of the flatiron building in New York City, except this one is round! A plaque on the façade of number 33 notes that Conrad Kickert lived and worked in that building from 1937 until his death in 1965, which makes him the longest living non-Frenchman on that street that I know of. About Umberto Brunelleschi I know nothing other than he lived at number 22 in 1912. The Symbolist poet and editor of the journal *Vers et Prose*, Paul Fort, lived during the decade preceding 1914 at number 24, not far from his dear friends, the Diriks.

Look into the end of the 17, rue Campagne-Première alley of studios and see if the spray-painted graffiti reading "Elvis tu es mort!" still decorates the white wall.

*****

At the end of the street, turn left and continue down the Boulevard Raspail, past the cemetery to the Place Denfert-Rochereau and look to the southeast, you will see the broad Boulevard Saint-Jacques. In 1891, after studying with Thomas Eakins at the Pennsylvania Academy of Fine Arts, the young painter, **Henry Ossawa Tanner**, left Philadelphia for Paris to refine his technique and live in what he hoped would be a more liberated, less racist society. Whether or not he obtained the latter may

41

be questionable, but he certainly achieved the former, beginning with winning a medal at the 1897 Paris Salon for "The Raising of Lazarus," before he died in the city in 1937. His work deserves to be better known: several of his paintings are in the permanent collections of the Philadelphia Museum of Art and the National Museum of American Art in Washington DC, including works resulting from his trips to North Africa and Palestine, and a very curiously posed Salomé from around 1900 done in various shades of blue and white, simultaneously threatening and erotically magnetic, a perfect Oscar Wilde-Richard Strauss emasculating vamp.

For most of his 46 years in Paris, a duration equalled by few non-French Parisians (for example, Gertrude Stein lived here for 42 and Alice Toklas for 57 years, and their friend Picasso lived there for approximately 50 years before moving permanently to the South, while the ever-eccentric Raymond Duncan spent more than 50 years in the city), Tanner had a studio at 51, boulevard Saint-Jacques. From 1906 to 1912, he also had a studio at 70bis, rue Nôtre-Dame-des-Champs. He deserves a plaque on the wall of the Boulevard Saint-Jacques building.

Tanner's painting, "The Raising of Lazarus," attracted the attention of whichever official government Frenchman administered the painting budget and the government purchased it in 1897 for the Musée du Luxembourg, an act which lent tremendous prestige to Tanner, and, one hopes, gave him deep satisfaction. Booker T. Washington, himself, in 1899, visited Tanner and published an appreciation of the artist that may have been more politically oriented than aesthetically motivated. Nonetheless, Washington seems to have grasped, as much as he repressed its darker meaning, that this recognition of a Negro painter could not have occurred in the USA. He wrote, "Here in France no one judges a man by his color," which is, of course, not true, then or now, especially now. By 1904, "The Raising of Lazarus" had marched into the Louvre, but apparently marched back to his studio again because, apparently, it hung there in 1925 and 1929. I must admit I am not sure where it is now, but in 1969 it apparently belonged "to the Musée d'Art Moderne and has been stored at Compiègne." In 1906, the French government purchased another of Tanner's works, "The Disciples at Emmaüs," which they lost at some point during the 1939-1945 Era of Evil Tidings.

In 1928, Countee Cullen rented an apartment on the Avenue du Parc Montsouris for his new wife and himself in order to be near his friend Tanner. Cullen made annual trips to Paris and he continued to visit Tanner until the latter's death. One would much like to know that about which they talked! Perhaps not so curiously, Tanner's name appears in none of the memoirs of the "expatriate 1920s." Perhaps, indeed, his mentalité and his art were too conservative for the young, white avant-garde. Even Nancy Cunard had nothing to say about him. However, in 1969, the University of Chicago Press published Marcia Mathews' biography entitled *Henry Ossawa Tanner, American Artist*; Dewey Mosby published a longer biography in 1991, and there have been several exhibitions of his work in the last twenty years or so.

Tanner died at peace in his sleep on May 25, 1937, in his apartment at 43, rue de Fleurus, and is buried beside his beloved wife, Jessie, in the cemetery at Sceaux, a Parisian suburb where they owned a summer house.

The French government awarded three black Americans the Legion of Honor, Henry O. Tanner (1923), Joséphine Baker (1961), and James Baldwin (1986), all of them so honored before the award became debased in the 1990s.

Of course there have been other black American artists who studied, worked and exhibited in Paris. These include, for example, Palmer Hayden (1890-1973), whose extreme images of urban Negro life caused controversy then and now, and William Henry Johnson (1901-1970), who also lived for many years in Denmark with his Danish ceramist wife and whose deliberately primitively styled images, a large collection of which are in the National Museum of American Art in Washington, unfortunately continue to raise questions about his talent.

Lois Mailou Jones (1905-), probably the only American Negro woman painter to achieve success and fame abroad during the 1930s and 1940s, studied at the Académie Julian during 1937-1938, living in a studio at 23, rue Campagne-Première, when she exhibited at several of the salons. In 1952 a book containing 100 of her paintings done in France appeared, appropriately enough, in France. Ms Jones spent 47 years (1930-1977) teaching at Howard University in Washington DC. The Corcoran Gallery

Henry Ossawa Tanner, a fine though conservative American painter, had a studio for more than twenty years at 51, boulevard Saint-Jacques. The French awarded Tanner the Legion of Honor medal; now the city should put an appropriate plaque on the wall of the building.

of Art housed a retrospective of her work in honor of her 89th birthday in 1994 and a large-format book devoted to her life and art appeared in the same year.

Beauford Delaney (1902-1977), a friend of James Baldwin (he appears in at least one of the documentary films about Baldwin) and the subject of an essay by Henry Miller, who met him in the early 1940s in Greenwich Village ("The Amazing and Invariable Beauford Delaney"), began exhibiting in New York City in 1930 and moved permanently to Paris in 1953, where he continued to paint and encourage young black artists in their work. Mental illness clouded his last years during which he ceased painting entirely. His life and work deserve a comprehensive study.

Archibald John Motley, Jr. (1891-1981) spent the 1929-1930 year studying in Paris on a Guggenheim Fellowship, which he received after winning the 1928 Harmon Foundation gold medal for fine arts. At least one of his Paris paintings is in the Schomberg Center collection in New York City.

William Edouard Scott (1884-1964) trained in the classical techniques of oil painting at the Art Institute of Chicago and then spent the years 1909 to 1911 in Paris studying with French teachers and with Henry O. Tanner. In 1918, he returned to France with an apparently official commission to make drawings of Negro soldiers in action, several of which subsequently appeared on the cover of *The Crisis*, a journal edited by W.E.B. DuBois.

Laura Wheeler Waring (1887-1948) travelled in Europe and North Africa on a scholarship in 1914 and stopped in Paris before the diplomats, newspapers and military officials extinguished the lamps of Europe at the end of August. In 1924, she returned to Paris to study for a year at the Académie de la Grande Chaumière. Hale Aspacio Woodruff (1900-1980) studied at the Académie Scandinave and the Académie Moderne during 1927-28 and remained in France until 1931 when he returned to the USA to teach at Atlanta University.

Albert Alexander Smith (1896-1940) presents an interesting situation: according to the entry in *Against All Odds: African American Artists and the Harmon Foundation* (1989), after studying at the Ethical Culture Art School and the National Academy of Design, whereafter he became quite well-known and respected for his prints, he moved to France in 1928 to work as an entertainer in the cabarets and to continue to pursue his printmaking and engraving. The entry is illustrated by three examples of his work, one of which, an etching entitled "Market, Nice" is dated 1925, which makes one wonder if he imagined the scene or if the date of his arrival in France is wrong. (Unfortunately this is not the only such anomaly in the book.) Smith died in Paris in 1940. What occupied his time and talents during those years? Where in Paris did he live? What was the nature of his relationship with Tanner, of whom he made a portrait? With whom did he pal around in Paris? What was his life like in the city, especially as war approached? Under what circumstances and in what month did he die? Before or after the Germans occupied the city?

L'Entr'acte: Augusta Savage, Janet Scudder, Malvina Hoffman, Meta Warrick Fuller, and Elizabeth Prophet

The sculptor Augusta Savage (1900-1962) lived and worked for some time in Paris. She not only possessed a remarkable name, but also considerable talent. If what remains of her sculptures is any indication, one of the great mishaps of the century is the loss, due to indifference and destruction, of the bulk of her work. In the New York Public Library's Schomberg Center for Research in Black Culture, her ironically titled piece "Gamin" (1930) sits, according to one source, unseen by those who might most benefit from exposure to this disturbing portrait of a young black boy, whose future might possibly be bright and successful, but the scepticism of his visage seriously considers his chances less than favorable. White liberals will experience wrenching guilt when they look upon the six-inch darkened plaster (no, not bronze, there's never been enough money for that); black Americans today may be forgiven for wondering, when they see the statue, when, not if, the boy went out into the street with fire in his eyes and a gun in his hand. A photograph of the bust appears in *Harlem Renaissance: Art of Black America* (1987), and C. S. Rubenstein's reference book, *American Women Artists from Early Indian Times to the Present* (1982), devotes a few paragraphs to her in addition to a photograph of one of the magnificent, but destroyed sculptures she made for the 1939 New York World's Fair. Once again, no money could be found to cast the plaster in bronze.

Since writing the above paragraph, I've found a source informing us that a nine-inch high bronze of "Gamin" dated 1929 is in the permanent collection of Howard University's Gallery of Art in Washington DC, as is the bronze "La Citadelle - Freedom." Photographs of these pieces, as well as the painful "Green Apples" (1928), appear in *Against All Odds.*

One does not know much about Augusta Savage in Paris. Her name appears from time to time in Michel Fabre's book, *From Harlem to Paris Black American Writers in France 1840-1980* (1991), wherein she is praised for her work, but none of it is illustrated in the photographs. For several years in the 1930s she kept a studio on the Rue de Châtillon, or the Avenue de Châtillon as Fabre indicates, in the southern reaches of the 14th arrondissement. It is possible that what is now Avenue Jean Moulin was Avenue de Châtillon before 1964. In any case, both are southwest of the Place Victor Basch and the Alésia métro station.

Augusta Savage applied to become a student at the Palais de Fontainebleau summer art school in 1922, or 1923 depending on the source. School officials rejected her application, evidently thinking that white parents would not send their daughters to a class with a black girl as a classmate. Miss Savage fought with bitter determination to have the rejection overturned; with the support of public personalities, such as W.E.B. DuBois, she pursued the issue in the major newspapers and weekly magazines. It is not clear from the sources I've read whether she succeeded or not, but the hostility the campaign engendered in the white, male museum and art dealer world made it impossible for her to earn a living from her sculptures, and she worked for years in factories and laundries to pay the rent and eat. In 1929, or 1930 depending on the source, the Julius Rosenwald Foundation and the Carnegie Foundation gave her a series of fellowships to study at the Académie de la Grande Chaumière. She returned to New York in 1931, or 1932 depending on the source, where she became deeply involved with administering school programs for young Harlem artists; indeed her own work suffered from lack of attention as she concentrated on assisting others. Her last major exhibition occurred in 1939 at the Augusta Savage Studios in Harlem, whereafter she apparently withdrew for the final twenty years of her life to a small upstate town. It is not surprising, but nonetheless intensely sad to read that "few of her works from the 1920s and 1930s have been located."

Janet Scudder (1869-1940), who also received the Legion of Honor award, belongs to an earlier generation of American women who struggled against male spite and resistance to their work. General information on this sculptor is easier to come by than that about Miss Savage, if only because Miss Scudder and the Misses Gertrude Stein and Alice Toklas developed a lasting friendship while they all lived in Paris before and after the 1914-1918 phase of the Great 20th Century Idiocy. Consequently, Miss Scudder appears flittingly in the various Stein-Toklas biographies. She published a book of memoirs called *Modeling My Life* in 1925, but this is out of print and difficult to locate.

In Chicago as a young but strong-willed girl, Scudder saw the Frederick William MacMonnies fountain in the court of honor at the World Columbian Exposition in 1893 and decided then and there that she would study with him and become a sculptor. The next year she began work as his assistant in his Paris studio at 16, rue Antoine-Bourdelle, then called Impasse du Maine. She lived then at the American University Women's Paris Club, now Reid Hall, at 4, rue de Chevreuse (6th). The house and gardens may be visited, but not at all times and only with special permission, so be prepared for disappointment if you wish to follow Scudder's life in Paris.

You can at least walk by her former residence at 70 bis, rue Nôtre-Dame-des-Champs into which she moved in December 1924 after Ezra Pound and Dorothy Shakespear transferred their activities to Rapallo. Scudder thereafter moved to 24, rue de Verneuil (7th), which runs parallel to the Rue Jacob and the Seine north of the Boulevard Saint-Germain, where she continued to work in Paris and sell her pieces in New York City. She must have had a studio elsewhere during the period she spent in Pound's former apartment, which was barely large enough to hold the Pounds much less a sculptor's studio. That she continued to turn out her work is not in doubt: in the summer of 1932, at the age of 62, she participated in a Paris exhibition entitled "American Women's Show." In her *New Yorker* letter of June 22, 1932, Janet Flanner wrote that the works exhibited "showed an amazonian quality of strength that did not surprise or fail to please." Not quite a rave review, but sympathetic and appreciative nonetheless. Flanner's standards were rigorous, stringent and difficult to meet. The word "amazon" served during the period before 1939 as a codeword for lesbian.

According to James Mellow's *Charmed Circle: Gertrude Stein and Company* (1974), Scudder's "forte was pleasant and inoffensive garden statuary - prancing fauns, nubile girls, boys on dolphins." Veritable lawn toys. No wonder one of her principal buyers was Stanford White, the unfortunate architect, who commissioned her to make such things for estates he built on Long Island.

Miss Stein named her the "doughboy" because "there were only two perfectly solemn things on earth, the doughboy and Janet Scudder." According to Miss Stein, Miss Scudder had "all the subtlety of the dough-boy and all his nice ways and all his lonesomeness." Miss Stein approved less of Miss Scudder's "real pioneer's passion for buying useless real estate," but this is all gossip, required from time to time to loosen the ties that tend to bind, but tedious in the long run. Miss Scudder and her companion, Mrs. Camille Lane, did not buy a house in Grasse, but did take one in Aix-en-Provence, which did not work out, as Miss Stein had previously warned, and they returned to Paris.

Miss Scudder's work can be seen in the collections of the Metropolitan Museum of Art ("Frog Fountain"), the Peabody Institute in Baltimore ("Tortoise Fountain"), the Chicago Art Institute ("Fighting Boy Fountain," which brings to mind Alan Ladd standing on a box to reach Sophia Loren's height in *Boy on a Dolphin*, in which Miss Loren rises from the sea soaked in a thin blue dress in one of the most innocently erotic scenes on the American screen in the 1950s, the image of which became a popular poster in the mid-1960s), and the collections of many private, and to me unknown, estates.

Prior to August 1914, Miss Scudder held Saturday "afternoons" (not to conflict with Miss Stein's Saturday "evenings") in her studio at 1, rue de la Grande Chaumière (6th), where, it is said, Gordon Craig and Henry Adams might appear. Miss Scudder did not meet Malvina Hoffman (1887-1966) when the latter young lady moved with her mother briefly into a pension at 77, rue Nôtre-Dame-des-Champs in 1910. Miss Hoffman had met Miss Scudder earlier that year in Florence at Mabel Dodge's villa under unusual circumstances having to do with Miss Scudder's belief in ghosts. The interested reader is referred to Miss Hoffman's memoirs, *Yesterday is Tomorrow* (1965), for further details of the meeting. The younger woman called on the other, worked briefly as the latter's studio helper mixing clay and what-not, and one Saturday found herself saying hello to Miss Gertrude Stein amidst the Picassos, Cézannes and Matisses. All this in 1910.

The 23-year old Hoffman then rented a small studio at 72, rue Nôtre-Dame-des-Champs, her first with a northern exposure, presumably to be near the two academies of art, Académie de la Grande-Chaumière and the Académie Colarossi. Later that year, having pressured Rodin into reluctantly allowing her to be his assistant, a job she held on and off when in Paris until his death in 1917, she moved into a studio-apartment at 17, rue Campagne-Première (14th). The artist, William Stanley Hayter, lived at the same address in the 1930s, before the international crime syndicate called The Great Powers went to war again in 1939-40 and forced him to move to New York City with his etching business called, not surprisingly, "Atelier 17."

The French added Miss Hoffman's work "Russian Bacchanale" to the permanent collection in the Jardin du Luxembourg, but do not look for it now. The Germans melted down the bronze in 1941 to make artillery shells. Her first commission in Paris was for a bust of the US Ambassador to France, Robert Bacon, in 1910.

In 1927, Miss Hoffman purchased a plot of land at 25 Villa Santos-Dumont (15th), described as a "19th century alleyway," designed a three-storey house with large windows cut into the roof over her studio, oversaw its construction and moved into it the next summer. During the next ten years she worked with the same demonic strength of will she showed in forcing Rodin to recognize her as a serious artist. One of her pieces, "Bill Working," the French accessioned into the Jeu de Paume; it is presumably now in the Musée d'Orsay collection. She spent the war years in the United States and returned to Paris in 1948 to find her house dusty, but in perfect condition except for the garden which had grown rampant and wild.

Shortly after her return she sculpted a bust of Teilhard de Chardin, which the Ministry of Fine Arts purchased and, one assumes, added to the collections in the Musée National d'Art Moderne in the Centre Pompidou. She also sculpted the memorial for the United States military cemetery in Épinal in the Vosges. In 1961, at the age of 74, she sold the house. Browsing through her autobiography, *Heads and Tails* (1936), in addition to an earlier book mostly about her travels in the Near and Far East and Africa, is well worth the time for it is full of anecdotes, now amusing though perhaps less so when they occurred, such as how her tenacious persistence gained her the position as Rodin's assistant.

One cannot escape his presence if one considers sculpture during and surrounding the Belle Epoque in Paris. He encouraged the work of Meta Vaux Warrick Fuller (1877-1968) and accepted her as a student, which gave her immense prestige among those with any pretensions at being kulturny. Fuller needed both the encouragement and the association with Rodin, not because she lacked talent, quite the opposite in fact, but because she was an American black woman, and thus carried built-in disadvantages that had nothing to do with her abilities as an artist. In 1899, after graduating from the Pennsylvania School of Industrial Art, she won a scholarship to study in Paris, and searched for a room at the American Girls Club. The management refused, though she was both American and a girl; her problem of course lay in her color. No room at that inn, but Tanner, a fellow Philadelphian, found her a small, and one hopes well-heated, hotel room.

On the advice of Saint-Gaudens she enrolled in the École des Beaux-Arts and studied drawing for three years with Raphael Collin, in addition to studying at the Académie Colarossi with Injalbert and Rollard. In 1902 she exhibited some pieces and met Rodin at the Salon de l'Art Nouveau, the gallery owned by Siegfried Bing, who also published the influential review *Le Japon Artistique* (1888-91). In the following year, she exhibited "The Wretched" and "The Impenitent Thief" at the Paris Salon, and returned to Philadelphia to enroll in the Pennsylvania Academy of Fine

Arts. In 1939 she exhibited at the Augusta Savage Studios in New York.

Fuller was the first black American artist to make consistent use of American Negro and African motifs and forms, long before the Harlem Renaissance brought these to public notice. (However, Alain Locke credits the sculptor May Howard Johnson in the late 19th century with being the first to move into "frank and deliberate racialism" in Negro art.) Until Fuller began her professional career as a sculptor, only a few scattered images that could be described as African or American Negro existed in American high art. Curiously, Tanner, who normally worked in the white European mainstream both stylistically and in terms of content, painted two of these works ("Banjo Lesson" 1893 and "The Thankful Poor" 1894). Fuller created what is perhaps her most well-known piece, "Ethiopia Awakening" (now at the Schomberg Center in the 135th Street branch of the New York Public Library), in 1914, a pan-African work tying together black nationalism, a perceived if not historically accurate black Egyptian heritage, the emotions of motherhood and the idea of renaissance. Yes, I know this sounds pompous if not impossible, but I suggest you see the sculpture itself or at least the photograph of it (along with other Fuller work) in *Harlem Renaissance: Art of Black America*. You might also see the Danforth Museum of Art catalog, *An Independent Woman: Life and Art of Meta Warrick Fuller* (1985). I regret not having found any addresses for Fuller in Paris. Perhaps a future edition will have them.

Of the sculptress Nancy Elizabeth Prophet, even less is generally known than of the others discussed above. In the summer of 1929, Miss

Prophet exhibited her work in Paris and had tea on July 2 with Countee Cullen and other black Americans to celebrate the occasion. On August 2, 1929, the newspaper *Afro-American* published a gossipy article entitled "Beth Prophet Hailed as Artist in Paris."

And that paragraph contains all I knew myself at first, this sparse information found in a brief textual reference and a source note in, again, Fabre's book. All well and good for a throwaway reference in a short paragraph, but who was she? Why was she in Paris? Where had she come from and what became of her after Paris? And if I knew all this, would it be relevant to this book? Well yes, it would; so I slowly, when other pressures allowed, began to look for her life.

After a certain amount of frustration, best left undescribed here, I found a copy of *Against All Odds*, which contains the bare bones of information about her life, but barely; thus leaving one even more curious than previously. Her life would seem to be the stuff of melodrama, a particularly American melodrama.

Born in Providence, Rhode Island, in 1890, Miss Prophet graduated from the Rhode Island School of Design in 1918 and moved to France in 1922 at the age of 32, where she attended the École des Beaux-Arts, having better luck than Augusta Savage in that year, and exhibited in the Salons d'Automne, the August Salons and the Salon des Artistes Français to positive and encouraging reviews. *Against All Odds* tantalizingly but obscurely notes that despite her known "self-imposed isolation," she came to know W.E.B. DuBois, Henry Tanner and, as we know, Countee

Cullen, while she lived in Paris. DuBois introduced her to Augusta Savage when the latter arrived in the city and Miss Prophet may indeed have influenced some of Miss Savage's work at the time.

During her residence in Paris, Miss Prophet exhibited at the Rhode Island School of Design, the Boston Society of Independent Artists and the Harmon Foundation, the latter of which awarded her the 1929 (or 1930 depending on the source) Otto H. Kahn exhibition prize. She returned to the USA in 1932 where she taught at Spelman College in Atlanta, Georgia, until 1944 when she moved to Providence and held a final exhibition of her work in the public library, after which she apparently disappears into a life of poverty and obscurity. Miss Prophet died in 1960. The biographical text in *Against All Odds* notes "Upon her death, a funeral fund was raised to keep her from a pauper's burial." Raised by whom? What did she do during the last sixteen years of her life?

Where did Miss Prophet have tea with Cullen in July 1929? At what cafés did she drink an apéritif and heatedly discuss the questions of form and content, money and space to work, the eternal questions argued about by all artists at all times? Did she have her own studio? Where? Of what did this so-called "isolation" consist? Did the lightness of her skin color trouble her? Did she have a boyfriend or a girlfriend? On what Parisian streets did she pace back and forth agitated by those particular problems that confront the black artist regardless of geographical locus?

Fin de l'Entr'acte

The sculptor Antoine Bourdelle (1861-1929) created an extraordinary number of public pieces during his lifetime, some of which somehow were never placed in public places. These and many of his maquettes are to be seen in the **Musée Bourdelle**, at 16, rue Antoine-Bourdelle, a block northwest of the Gare Montparnasse. If he were alive, one could send his mail to him "dans sa rue," surely a very nice way to receive one's mail, a rare occurrence when one is alive, with Victor Hugo as an exception. Augustus Saint Gaudens, an American sculptor despite his name, had in 1878 a studio in this street, then named Impasse du Maine.

Jo Davidson, creator of the stolid Gertrude Stein stone image, among countless other busts, had a stone-cutting shop in the street during the 1920s, from which he visited Bourdelle's atelier from time to time. The Stein bust is prominently displayed in the National Portrait Gallery in Washington, which also holds many of Davidson's bread and butter bust portraits of politicians, industrialists and soldiers. In 1931, Davidson's monumental 16 feet (just over five meters) tall stone doughboy, originally intended for one of the American cemeteries in France, had to be demolished when the city enlarged the Impasse du Maine to create what is now the Rue Antoine-Bourdelle, necessitating the destruction of his studio and with it the huge figure: Davidson could not pay the cost of moving such a monolith.

In his memoirs, Davidson tells the possibly apocryphal story about walking to his studio in the Impasse du Maine with Aristide Maillol and passing Bourdelle, who ignored or snubbed them. According to Maillol's explanation of this unusual behavior, the two French artists had been friends since their youths when Maillol painted, before he began to sculpt. One day while waiting in Bourdelle's studio, Maillol started to model his own hand with some clay to pass the time. Bourdelle finally arrived and, furious at what he saw, yelled: "Il ne faut pas faire de la sculpture!" And they rarely spoke again, at least according to Maillol. Bourdelle had reason to fear Maillol's transferring his talents to sculpture.

❋❋❋❋

Alas, that gigantic erection to the worst of modern man's seemingly unquenchable thirst for power over the natural and human environment, **The Mean and Terrifically Ugly Montparnasse Tower**, literally overshadows Bourdelle's museum and everything else in the neighborhood. Its 55 stories in dark glass and grey concrete are a tribute to the worst, the basest of mankind's destructive acquisitive instincts. Here the 1985 green *Guide Michelin* to Paris suffers a rare lapse in discrimination: the drivel written about the Tour-Maine-Montparnasse, to give this inexcusable excrement its proper name, is on the level of Jackie Collins. Now in his ninth decade, Julien Green, member of the Académie, whom I have read with some admiration up to this point, has something seemingly positive to say about this ruthless act of barbarism in his recent collection of texts and photographs called *Paris* (1991). Perhaps Mr. Green loves too much of Paris too much. On the other hand, the passage in question is about a "refraction phenomenon" and "fiery windows" and "blazing pink," so the positive aspect of it might, perhaps, be interpreted in another way. Indeed, elsewhere in his slim volume, he writes of the "strange abomination" of the School of Medicine on the corner of Rue des Saints-Pères and Rue Jacob, whose "hideousness" constitutes an "outrage" in a city as beautiful as Paris. In deep bitterness Green suggests a paraphrase of an old Roman jibe against the Barberini family as an inscription over the School's portal: "What the Barbarians left undone, Parisians have finished." Green is obviously on the side of the angels in the end.

Franz Kafka's one-page story, "The City Coat-of-Arms," attributes to the unnamed, no doubt emblematic city a closed fist as the coat-of-arms. "All the legends and songs that come to birth in that city are filled with longing for a prophesied day when the city would be destroyed by five successive blows from a gigantic fist." The Centre Pompidou, La Défense, Euro-Disney, and the Montparnasse high-rise are harbingers of that day. In fear and trembling we await the Moloch-devilopers' final blow in the realization of Kafka's nightmare when Paris becomes, not *Alphaville*'s sterile wasteland of the spiritually moribund (the egregious Bibliothèque de France will ensure this), but the setting for *Blade Runner*'s stinking, acid-rained metropolis of the replicant living dead.

The relatively unknown American painter, Marsden Hartley, subleased a studio at 18, rue Moulin de Beurre, a street which is no longer there because the devilopers obliterated it to erect the Gare Montparnasse office complex connected with the tower. But in 1912, Hartley moved into a working class neighborhood far enough from the cafés and bars so that he could feel productively isolated and get his own work done. He appreciated the colorful attire of the workmen of the quarter in their "baggy corduroy trousers of light blue, dark brown and some wonderful rose color and wide sash belts of fiery red - big shoes - often sabots - and caps or hats." He also appreciated the workmen themselves, finding "some very handsome," as his biographer puts it. He seems to have done a considerable amount of work here, but the studio is dust and ashes.

The Netherlandish painter, Piet Mondrian, came to Paris in 1911 and visited his countryman, the artist Conrad Kickert in his studio at 26, rue du Départ. Kickert left the city for a while and lent the place to Mondrian, who stayed there and in another studio in the building for a number of years. He returned briefly in 1919, and in 1921 moved in for a stay of 15 years, whereafter he left Europe for New York. Mondrian, as one might expect from his geometric paintings with the vernacular titles ("Boogie-Woogie"), spent little time in the cafés due to an obsession with his work, the style of which reflected his living quarters, described by an unknown visitor cited by Arlen Hansen: the apartment showed "an order that was balanced and cunningly calculated beyond perfection, a few squares of yellow and red and blue against vast stretches of white. The gramophone was red, so was the table. The wardrobe was blue. The plates yellow. The curtains red...." A street with the same name is still there, but do not look for a building with studios at number 26: the Montparnasse tower brutally dominates the entire block in all its fascist machoisme.

Sic transit gloria mundi.

Actually, the hideous tower is in the 15th arrondissement, but it looms implacably, inescapably, threateningly, over a large part of the 14th, which is our concern here. One feels positively compelled to hurry along to the Montparnasse cemetery where one can pretend the despicable monster doesn't exist, if one doesn't look up to the west.

❋❋❋❋

The **Cimetière de Montparnasse**, officially named the Cimetière du Sud, is located south of the Boulevard Montparnasse and walkable from the Café du Dôme. The concierge maintains in his hut, at the Boulevard Edgar Quinet entrance, an "Index Sommaire des Célébrités," which is now sufficiently up to date to list Man Ray, and will have references to the designer of the Statue of Liberty (a smaller version of which can be seen below the Trocadéro on the Seine), Friedrich August Bartholdi, Baudelaire, de Maupassant, Jean Seberg, Alfred Dreyfus, Brancusi, Tristan Tzara, Sartre and de Beauvoir, Zadkine, Léon-Paul Fargue, et alia. The Index will not tell you that the American painter and diarist, Shirley Goldfarb, is buried here, but she is, as she wished to be. All in all, we think we, too, would rather be buried here than in Père Lachaise; in Montparnasse death is less crowded, if not quieter.

**L'Entr'acte: *The Paris Review*,
H. L. Humes, *The Underground City***

At the outermost edge of the southwestern quadrant of the cemetery, walk into the mouth of the Rue de l'Ouest for one block and turn right into the tiny Rue de Perceval just off the Rue Vercingétorix (what a name! reminds me of a comic book), and stop in front of number 14. You will be looking at the building in which, on a bright warm afternoon in the Spring of 1952, a small group of young American writers and friends made plans to launch one of the most important literary journals of the latter half of the 20th century, *The Paris Review*.

This coterie acted in a tradition which included hundreds of known and obscure "little magazines" published in various forms for hundreds of years and, in the 20th century, many of them in English in Paris. Elsewhere in this book I have written a bit about *transition*, but there are dozens that could be mentioned such as *Zéro, Broom, Points, Contact,* Pound's *The Exile, The Little Review* (banned in New York for publishing parts of *Ulysses* in 1919), *The Booster* later called *Delta* (under the brief "editorial direction" of Henry Miller, Alfred Perlès and Lawrence Durrell), *This Quarter, The Transatlantic Review, The New Review, Tambour, Gargoyle, Succession, Larus, The Boulevardier, Janus, Olympia, Frank, Merlin,* and ... Well. Some lasted only two or three issues, some lasted years. Two or three English language literary journals continue to be published in Paris today, but *The Paris Review* is not one of them; since the early 1970s, it has been published in New York City. The editors had, in the beginning, the aim of publishing creative work by young writers rather than acrid academic theorizing and ratiocinative criticism full of sticky cobwebs and the odor of drains. This standard the journal has continued to uphold.

The Montparnasse Cemetery.

The apartment belonged to Peter Matthiessen, whose guests that afternoon included John Train, Thomas Guizburg, William Pène du Bois, George Plimpton, William Styron and Harold L. Humes. Mattiessen and Humes, who had met at the Café du Dôme in early 1951, wanted to publish a real literary journal to print the work of writers too good for Humes' current rag called *News-Post*, a curiously hybrid magazine containing gossip and recommendations for places to eat and other crepuscular activities. Matthiessen describes Humes as "burly and curly... with a deep laugh... aggressive, warm-hearted, curious, yet with convictions on every subject... all of which made him impossible." In short, the kind of young man who amuses and challenges you in a saloon, but who you would not necessarily think of taking to your parents' house for dinner.

So by the Spring of 1952, they gathered a number of friends together with the young Plimpton, whom Matthiessen brought in from England to be editor-in-chief when it became clear that Humes, who originally appointed himself to that position, could not possibly deal with other people in a manner necessary to the successful management of a literary journal. On that sunny Spring day, energized by Plimpton's two bottles of absinthe, the group accepted the name of the magazine suggested by one of them and declared their readiness to surge forward into the world of publishing. But a name does not a publication make and the journal's founders roller-coasted through many months before the first issue saw the light of booksellers' windows and kiosk stands. The group made Humes managing editor because of his previous experience publishing *News-Post*, and actually expected him to manage the business, a responsibility he apparently found himself unable to fulfill due to the pressures of other matters demanding his attention.

Indeed, Plimpton tells what may be an apocryphal (but one hopes not!) story of Humes' reaction to being demoted on the masthead from managing editor to advertising and circulation manager. Not only did he not find the time to carry out his managing duties in Paris, being too occupied with reading *Huckleberry Finn* at the Rotonde and working on the novel which would become *The Underground City*, one of the great unknown American masterpieces of the latter half of the 20th century, but he moved to New York City before the first issue appeared! When the copies of the inaugural issue reached the docks of New York and Humes discovered his demotion, he immediately acted to write the wrong. A letter of complaint to his fellow editors, however elegantly written, would not do, it could be ignored. Humes purchased a rubber stamp engraved with his name and his more prestigious original title, and a red ink pad. Racing to the wharf, he tore into the crates containing the magazine and, wildly wielding both items, stamped the masthead page of 500 or so issues "before his arm got tired."

Perhaps Humes was simply difficult to get along with, eh? *The Underground City* shows a twisting, labyrinthian mind which cannot stop making connections (far beyond Morgan Forster's desperate command), but in the end there is a diamond-like lucidity which is both charming and honest, demanding space and time to narrate the unnarratable without exhortation or vulgar psychoanalysis.

By the way, as one historian says to another, according to Barnaby Conrad III in his book, *Absinthe: History in a Bottle* (1988), the French government banned the wormwood-based drink on March 16, 1915, and the Swiss in 1907 made it illegal to distill, sell or transport the stuff, but not to drink it! In Spain, absinthe manufacture is still legal and perhaps that is the source of Plimpton's, or it might have been bootlegged, or may have even been pastis - who knows, and it does not really matter: we shall continue to think of it as absinthe.

Everyone who reads American literature knows William Styron; many who watch American television commercials know George Plimpton; this is as it should be. But which of you knows H. L. Humes, author of *The Underground City* (1958) and *Men Die* (1960)? I no longer remember the source of the money, savings perhaps, though I possessed little enough of that living in a Greenwich Village tenement in 1959, but I clearly remember buying the 755 page *Underground City*, the title referring in one sense to Paris, in another to the depths of men's minds and spirits where loyalty and betrayal are, often unconsciously, formulated, tested and reformulated. I clearly remember rushing back to the fourth floor flat a few blocks south of Washington Square in the American underground city.

I also clearly remember reading for days until I finished it, not quite getting it all, but reeling under the impression it made. It begins and ends in the rain in Paris after the war; the bulk of the action takes place in the south of France during the 1943-44 period of German occupation in which the American OSS agent named Stone confronts a complexity of life for which he is not fully prepared. A Jamesian situation acted out, not in the drawing rooms and gardens of the haute-bourgeoisie, but in the moral and spiritual miasma of war and sudden death. For some reason I did not read the second and last novel, or I no longer remember it. This is sadly appropriate since the first is really about memory and how one remembers chosen fragments and must learn to remember the others under terms of intense pressure and disgrace. The book also shows how politics can wreck decent men and women, who fought the complex underground war of resistance and collaboration, sacrificing them in the power struggle, according to the exigencies of the time, when behavior and ideas supported and reinforced during the war were made to seem as exemplars of betrayal and criminality after the war. It is not an easy book, and no doubt it is too long, but the cumulative effect of its narrative drive and character delineation breaks through the lines of critical defense to take the high ground of the art of fiction: the extremes of human behavior contained in a massive epiphany encompassing the variety of human experience.

The jacket cover is basically blue, shading upward from almost black at the bottom to almost sky-blue at the top; the Eiffel tower rises out of the primeval darkness toward the light, assuring reader-identification with the correct city and foretelling the essentially masculine tone of the book. A third of the way down, a thin red line runs horizontally across the cover, the spine, and the back, which mirrors the front. I think of the red line as the American agent's conscience, dignity and loyalty to his comrades and the truth as he knew it. A long book, a heavy book, with its epigrams from *Ulysses* (Stephen Dedalus on history and God) and Cristóbal Colón, Grand Admiral of the Ocean Seas ("There live the happiest people, who only die of weariness of living"); a book which, somewhere in my peregrinations about the western Eurocentric world, I mislaid.

With some certainty I can say that I did not think of Humes or the book for over twenty years. The gods who guide our destinies may know what triggered the memory several years ago when I began to think of the book again, perhaps wondering if it actually had to do with Paris and France, or if my memory misled me and the underground city was, in fact, Odessa. I started looking for the distinctive cover, which I did remember, in second hand bookstores, those idiosyncratic establishments that ineluctably draw me on almost as intensely as das ewige Weibliche. Some time later, in a Washington suburb known for its country clubs (restricted) and its "actual" 1940s diner (unrestricted, open all night), blessed with the goodluck-charm presence of my brother Dean, I found an almost mint copy and my heart soared simultaneously back to New York City in 1959 and forward to Key West where Lynn-Marie and I would soon spend a warm, sunny week of rest during which time I could again devour the book, testing my memory, and scratching the itch of curiosity.

The book knocked me out again, if this time for somewhat different reasons, coming to it now so much older if not so much wiser, perhaps looking for different things in the nuances of narrative, political ideology

70

and poetic voice. I had not remembered the amazing amount of stuff Humes crammed into the book, most of which fit, some of which stuck out awkwardly. It is a young man's book, but a young man oddly middleaged with too much knowledge of certain things and more than his share of cynicism. The war and its disappointing aftermath did that to some of the best creative minds.

At the end of September 1992, I pondered how I could reasonably inject into the book you are now reading a few paragraphs of appreciation of Humes, and a handful of other writers I think of as forming a loose association; that is to say, I associate them together for reasons of my own and see a connection which surely exists only in my own mind. Then Dean sent me a clipping from the *New York Times*, the headline of which said "Harold Louis Humes, 66, Novelist And a Paris Review Co-Founder." The piece obviously came from the obituary page. Immobilized for several moments, I finally read the text and discovered certain things I had not known about this man who had exercised my mind for such a long period of time. Why, for instance, had he not published anything of note after 1960? Apparently he told his family that "mental illness" had caused him not to finish his third novel. The obituary is tantalizingly incomplete: in 1973 Humes moved to Boston and Cambridge (where had he been since 1952?); he played chess in Harvard Square (did he, ahem, have "private means"?); he participated in "unorthodox activities" including founding a community service organization called Unidentified Flying Idea. He is survived by five daughters and one son, Malcolm Einaudi of Turin, Italy.

What had he done all those years besides siring children? What was the nature of the "mental illness" that blocked the work of what was clearly one of the major writers of his generation? Did he work as a plumber over those long years since Paris and Harvard (class of 1954), a watchmaker, a teacher of Latin in a prep school? Why is his son's name Einaudi? (Is that any of our business? Perhaps not, but the seductive temptress Curiosity is difficult to resist.)

With some research in the Library of Congress down the street, a few letters to Styron and Plimpton and others, perhaps one could answer these intrusive questions. But why now? Twenty years and more passed before I found *The Underground City* again. I have some hope that I will not require that amount of time to find *Men Die*. One of these days I will discover some of the answers about the enigma of Harold Humes, but the quest does not have to be pursued with a young man's intense enthusiasm and relentless energy. It is no longer a matter of patience, for I am not a patient man, but rather one of exhaustion and the acceptance of delayed satisfaction.

Should you walk past 14, rue de Perceval, stop for just a moment, raise your eyes to the third floor and briefly think of that group of young men, sure of themselves and their ability to make a difference to literature, to achieve their ends without compromising their standards, and wonder for a fleeting few seconds whether Harold Humes drank his absinthe with carbonated or non-carbonated water, or neat, strained through a sugar-cube.

Those other writers I referred to above are not those involved in founding *The Paris Review*, but three men whose novels are about America and Americans and the defining characteristics of parts of the country and the majority of its citizens at various times. This is what separates them from Humes' book, which has an American as the main character and is in part about America in terms of the nefarious American influence in Europe during the nascence of The Cold War, but is really Jamesian in the confrontation of the American with European culture. However, it is post-Jamesian in the ambiguity of mid-20th century notions of the dichotomy of good and evil, and who might clearly represent which, a matter no longer as transparent as it seemed to some in James himself.

Thomas Heggen wrote his first and only novel, the obviously autobiographical *Mr. Roberts* (1946), and worked on the very successful stage version of the book before he died under circumstances which might lead one to suspect suicide. Ross Lockridge, Jr. wrote what is argueably The Great American Novel, *Raintree County* (1948), after which he killed himself. Lockridge spent the academic year 1933-34 in Paris as a nineteen year-old student, first in the Rue Soufflot (which runs from the Panthéon to the Jardin du Luxembourg) with a family, and for the last few months of his year abroad in a room in the Rue d'Ulm. Here he experienced a vision of the story of America, told in the form of an Indiana family saga of two or three generations, to encompass the entire bodacious scope of the American Republic in war and peace, love and death, humor and democracy, with the Civil War as the crucible through which the characters and the Nation pass, none unscathed.

73

In Paris he also listened to lectures at 14, rue de la Glacière, the American student exchange organization headquarters. He excelled in his studies and learned a fine amount of French, wore a beret and muffler, and lost his virginity, finding the whole matter distasteful: midwestern morality defeated Parisian sophisticated naturalness. Indeed, France apparently had very little effect on the man and writer he became. The unusual technical narrative devices he used in *Raintree County* had already been used by Joyce and John Dos Passos, another author who spent time in Paris during the 1920s and 1930s and who wrote a profoundly American novel about America entitled *USA*, which, having moved himself politically from the left to the right, he later denigrated, but that is another story for another place. In 1974, John Leggett published a dual biography of Heggen and Lockridge called *Ross and Tom: Two American Tragedies*, which attempts to clarify the relationship between these two men and Scott Fitzgerald's notion that in American lives there is no second act. Lockridge's son, Larry, has recently published a lengthy biography of his father (1994).

After publishing *The Ox-Bow Incident (1940)*, Walter Van Tilberg Clark wrote the autobiographical *The City of Trembling Leaves* (1945), which harkens back to Booth Tarkington, not of *Penrod and Sam*, but *The Magnificent Ambersons*, and Hamlin Garland's memoirs of the Middle Border. Van Tilberg Clark did not kill himself, but went on to write other books including *The Track of the Cat* and *The Watchful Gods*.

All these books and their authors are all tied together in my mind; I am not completely sure I understand why. I do know, however, that you will be a better human being if you read them. And you will enjoy doing so.

In any case, of all these writers only Harold Humes wrote a book with Paris as the setting and, of them, only he drank absinthe in the apartment in the Rue de Perceval that Spring day in 1952.

Fin de l'Entr'acte

The Boulevard Edgar Quinet obliquely borders the cemetery on its northern edge. If you stand in front of number 31 you will see a nondescript building devoted to the arts of medicinal cures. This was the first building in France to have air-conditioning; how French that it was a whorehouse! Called **Le Sphinx**, the only brothel in Montparnasse, opened with a bang, so to speak, in the late 1920s (or 1930, depending upon the source) under the efficient management of Marthe "Martoune" Lemestre, matronly and always dressed in black, who sent out invitations to the inaugural night that included wives and companions (or "mistresses," as we formerly called them). Half the artists and writers in the quarter, real and would-be, received the notices, and apparently all of them showed up to guzzle the free champagne, if not nuzzle the unfree service, and view the rooms upstairs, which housed a wide range of implements and styles to satisfy the broadest spectrum of tastes and desires.

The downstairs decor became famous and rivalled that of La Coupole, until then the most brilliant chromium and glass art deco lounge-bar interior in Paris. While the upstairs workrooms contained rather less decoration (Samuel Putnam said "[T]here was a connotation of Grand Rapids rather than the new functionalism - although the inevitable bidet was functional enough," but he's an American and what do they know about bordellos), the bar americain and salon on the groundfloor attracted, and the house encouraged, even those who wished only to have a drink, chat with friends, and ogle the barebreasted girls, to whom the management gave annual paid vacations. Having broken with the traditional heavy plush fabric decor de la maison close, the Sphinx allowed men to bring their wives and children to the public rooms: a café is a café even if it is in a whorehouse.

Alberto Giacometti said, "It was for me a place more marvelous than any other." Signor Giacometti also said, "Whores are the most honest girls. They present the bill right away. The others hang on and never let you go." Others might not find that so oppressive.

Another foreigner who lived for many years in Paris, albeit as a Jewish refugee, Erwin Blumenfeld, alleges that the French Interior Minister, Albert Sarraut, and his brother owned a part of the Sphinx. Sarraut, whose ministry controlled the national police, proved to be no friend of refugees when the Germans invaded France.

The open market on Boulevard Edgar-Quinet dominated by the Tour
Maine-Montparnasse.

Putnam, who attended the opening with his wife, called Le Sphinx "nothing if not respectable," and after the liberation, in April 1946, perhaps under the pecksniff morality of Mme de Gaulle, the National Assembly in a paroxysm of faux vertu passed a law closing the bordellos and the building became a dormitory for students at the Sorbonne. Klüver and Martin's book has a photograph of the salon and several of the staff which will give you some idea of the "egyptian" motif of the decor.

Somewhere on this street existed in the same time period an intimate bar called **Le Monocle** where lesbians could feel at ease and enjoy themselves without being on show, reputed to have been as famous in its day as Le Sphinx. This too is gone, but Brassaï's book, *The Secret Paris of the 1930s*, has several photographs of the place and its clients. In April 1996, a night spot called Le Monocle, at 60, boulevard Edgar Quinet, advertised itself as a "bar, cabaret féminin...striptease..." with drinks starting at 100 francs. Someone clearly did some historical research.

The Closerie des Lilas, bent under the weight of the city's cultural history, at 171, boulevard du Montparnasse at the juncture with Rue Nôtre-Dame-des-Champs, Boulevard Saint-Michel, Avenue de l'Observatoire, and Rue d'Assas, on the Place Camille Jullian.

The fabled Café du Dôme, about which no book exists that we know of, though everyone mentions drinking or eating there, including us. In earlier times, the sidewalk tables and chairs were not enclosed.

Across the street from the Dôme is La Rotonde, where one can sit of an evening and watch the promenading people whilst enjoying an apéritif in a famous watering hole.

Le Select, down the Boulevard from La Rotonde, remains a favorite of tourists, especially American, so the serendipity of Philippe Simon's photograph is appropriate.

Studios in the courtyard of 9, rue Campagne-Première in which lived, played, and worked Per and Lucy Krohg, the dueling painter Léopold Gottlieb, Walter Pach, and Martin Kaelin.

In one or another of these studios in the building complex at 17, rue Campagne-Première, Malvina Hoffman, William Stanley Hayter, Mina Loy, Rainer Maria Rilke, Mathilde Vollmöller, and hundreds of unknown others lived and worked, and still do.

A ground-floor studio in the courtyard of 8, rue de la Grande Chaumière. Nina Hamnett and her lover, the painter Waclaw Zawadowski (called Zawado) lived off this courtyard for several years from 1920, as did Paul Gauguin (1893-94), Alphonse Mucha (1893-96), Amedeo Modigliani and Jeanne Héburterne (1917-20). The building complex is now called L'Atelier Modigliani, which should surprise no one.

A favorite loitering spot: the bookstore *Les Nourritures Terrestres* at 129, boulevard du Montparnasse.

Index

Why, the reader may well ask, have an index, which is also a glossary, for such a slim volume as this? First, because it might be useful to some readers to be able to go directly to a specific topic; second, because it will help those who wish immediately to see if the author has covered all those subjects which the reader thinks should be covered in an essay on the 14th arrondissement; third, because I find indexes fun to construct; fourth, indexes can hold much of that stuff vitally important to the author (and thus for the reader as well) for which he can find no other place in the main text; and, fifth, because indexes can be entertainments of sorts in themselves.

One of the longest of these latter is Georges Perec's 58 page index to his great bulk of a 579 page tome *Life A User's Manual* (1987) (*La Vie mode d'emploi* [1978]), a post-modern equivalent to the greatest earlier 20th century literature, a reversal of Laurence Sterne's digressive *Tristram Shandy* style, a mathmetician's dream, a delightful example of game theories, an exemplar of Wagnerian Leitmotiven, a secondary source for the author's friends who wish to find their camouflaged selves, the glorious result of a tremendous creative effort, and what must have been a hellishly challenging job of translation. Respect and admiration to David Bellos, who also wrote a lengthy life of the short-lived Perec. Perec is an acquired taste, but one might keep in mind Italo Calvino's comment that *La vie mode d'emploi* is "the last real 'event' in the history of the novel," a view that presupposes the novel did not end with *Ulysses* and one upon which one might hang one's hope that there may be vital life yet left in that old flagship of the seas of world literature: is the "last" really "final"? Is the novel really dead? Surely not; it is mutating, which is not only inevitable, but perhaps, like the seasons, cyclical, eventually to return to Homer and the oral storytellers, where it began.

The best way to read this index for simple enjoyment is to put the recording "Serge Reggiani à l'Olympia" (1983) on the hi-fi machine, pour yourself a large balloon of chilled Tavel rosé, and let the combination take you away.

Abbott, Berenice (1898 Springfield, Ohio - 1991 Monson, Maine) great American photographer, savior of Eugène Atget's life's work, 6, 38-39,

Absinthe a forbidden schnapps alleged to rot brain cells at a certain level of consumption, 66, 68, 72, 75

Académie Colarossi well-known art school; established 1870, 4-5, 7, 31, 53, 55, 101, 115

Académie Julian a substantial art school; established 1873 by Rodolphe Julian, who made a fortune from his art-factories, which prepared students for the École des Beaux-Arts or for the Salon exhibition; students included George Moore, Jacques-

Émile Blanche, Bonnard, Vuillard, Matisse, Lipchitz, Derain and Léger, though many rebelled against the Classicist training offered here, 44, 96, 115, 126

Académie de la Grande Chaumière also a well-known art school; established 1904 or 1906, depending on the source, surprisingly still with us, 6, 47, 50, 53

Académie Matisse (1908 - 1912) opened as an attempt to create a source of income for the artist, he soon grew tired of it; apparently only Matisse and three other students spoke French at the school, the student bodies were otherwise all foreigners, many of whom were Jews, a matter of public concern to the more anti-semitic French critics of the time, a fact not terribly surprising considering both the existing climate of opinion in France and the fact that a large number of Jews from Eastern Europe and San Francisco inhabited Montparnasse and interested themselves in painting and other art forms, for enlightenment about which the reader is referred to the fine catalog entitled *The Circle of Montparnasse: Jewish Artists in Paris 1905-1945* (New York: Universe Books and The Jewish Museum, 1985), 4

Académie Moderne a less well-known art school; opened after 1918 in a studio adjoining 86, rue Nôtre-Dame-des-Champs, 47

Académie Scandinave a rather thoroughly unknown art school, 47

Académie Suisse (1815-1870) not so well-known predecessor to the Académie Colarossi, about whose students Camille Pissarro wrote to his son, Lucien, "...there were students who were remarkably skillful and could draw with surprising sureness. Later on I saw these same artists at work; they were still skillful, but no more than that. Just think of Bastien-Lepage! and Carolus-Duran!!! No, no, no, that is not art." 5, 96

Adams, Henry Brooks (1838 Boston - 1918 Washington DC) a rather morbid American intellectual with a well-known education, 53

Adjani, Isabelle (b. 1955 Paris) brilliant portrayer of disturbed women and some who are simply sexy, 33

Ahlers-Hestermann, Friedrich (1883 Hamburg, Germany - 1973 Berlin) German painter in Paris before 1914; fired by the nazis from his position as professor at the Cologne School of Painting; spent the years 1938-45 in Berlin, 10

Algren, Nelson (né Nelson Algren Abraham 1909 Detroit, Michigan - 1981 Sag Harbor, New York) American writer who remained for decades enraged at a lover who wrote about their affair; author of *The Man With the Golden Arm* (1949), 94

Alphaville (1965) cinematic vision of a robotic but clean future in which the hero drives a 1964 white Mustang through the empty streets of Paris, 61

Amazon codeword for lesbian in certain wide circles of cultured mental competents,

American Girls' Club see Reid Hall

American Mercury a former periodical, 15

American University Women's Paris Club see Reid Hall

Apollinaire, Guillaume (né Wilhelm Apollinaris de Kostrowitzki 1880 Rome - 1918 Paris) a much better poet than an art critic, though his publicity for the cubist works of Braque and Picasso proved important in putting the genre over; a good friend of the lovely Max Jacob; a major participant in The Great 1908 Rousseau Honor Banquet in Picasso's studio, 127

Apollonian-Dionysian Duality, The Old the Nietzschean structure found to be of use by a generation of cultural critics, 29

Aragon, Louis (1897 Paris-Neuilly - 1982 Paris) a one-time Surrealist writer of considerable talent who allowed his politics to corrode his credibility and censor his work; a French Stalinist, but also a resistant; his long love affair and marriage with the equally Stalinist Elsa Triolet is so well known that even *Paris-Match* took note of it; his novel *Le Paysan de Paris* (1926)- translated for some reason as *The Nightwalker* (1970) - written before his political commitment, is a marvelous evocation of the city, 36-37,

Asch, Nathan (1902 Warsaw - 1964 Mill Valley, California?) an under-published American writer who knew a thing or two about Paris toilets; whose story "Sammy" appeared in the January 1934 issue of *Die Sammlung*, a German exile journal edited by Klaus

Mann and Fritz Landshoff; his novel *The Office* was published in 1925, a year before *The Sun Also Rises*; Asch admired Hemingway who helped him revise a story for the *Transatlantic Review*, but the latter clearly viewed him as a competitor in the mid-1920s; one night, probably in 1924, on the way to the Café du Dôme for coffee after dinner the two well-watered young men argued about which of them possessed more talent, a discussion that later required serious dental work for Asch and drove Hemingway, who always felt terrible guilt after knocking another man's teeth out, to appear at Asch's room in the Rue Campagne-Première late that night to apologize and admit that Asch possessed "more of everything than any of us," at least according to one source; Asch did say after Hemingway's death that "I hated the son-of-a-bitch and I loved him"; son of the once well-known writer Sholem, 14

Asch, Sholem (1880 Kutno, Poland - 1957 London) author who emigrated to the USA in 1914, but who wrote mostly in Yiddish, including a novel about Jesus of Nazareth called *The Nazarene* (1939), 92

Atget, Eugène (1857 - 1927 Paris) when Man Ray tried to teach him to use a Rolleiflex to make his working easier, he tried it and told the younger man, "Trop vite, enfin": "le snapshot" moved faster than he could think, he said, and he remained with his primitive equipment as he haunted the early morning streets of the city; in 1968 the Museum of Modern Art in New York purchased the bulk of his work called the Abbott-Levy Collection, 39, 115

Baker, Joséphine (1906 Saint Louis, Missouri - 1975 Paris) leader of a very complicated life who could shimmy better than your sister Kate, 44

Bal Bullier one of the best dance-halls in Paris; locale where lovers met; conveniently located close to the Closerie des Lilas; became a military quartermaster clothing depot in August 1914 as the Germans and others quickly departed Paris for military service or peaceful havens, of which there were more then than there were 25 years later when the human genius for inflicting various sorts of pain had more fully developed; no longer extant at 33, avenue de l'Observatoire, 5

Bal Nègre, Le bar and dance-hall formerly at 48, rue Blomet (15th), frequented by black workers from the French colonies; white artists and intellectuals found it during the craze for everything Negro during the 1920s when the place became très chic; scene of the 1928 Bal Ubu costume party, 120

Bald, Wambly (1902 Chicago, Illinois - ?) chronicler of English-speaking Montparnasse life in the *Chicago Tribune (Paris Edition* and its successor, the *New York Herald (Paris Edition)* column "La Vie de Bohème (As Lived on the Left Bank)" 1929-33, though officially he was a proofreader; contributor to Samuel Putnam's *New Review* and other expatriate "little magazines"; friend of Alfred Perlès and Henry Miller, in whose *Tropic of Cancer* he appears as Van Norden, after whom young Lawrence Durrell named his rowboat on Corfu, 103, 126

Baldwin, James (1924 Harlem, New York City - 1987 Saint-Paul de Vence, France) American writer and civil rights activist who lived many years in Paris, 44, 46

Balzac, Honoré de (1799 Tours, France - 1850 Paris) novelist, debtor and consumer of vast amounts of coffee, 8, 17, 28, 99

Bar Américain a generic drinking locale in France where one can, theoretically, if one is misguided enough, order a "cocktail," one of those dreadful, and by any sensible person dreaded, American-originated mixed drinks, which are guaranteed to ruin one's appetite and upset one's head, 76

Bartholdi, Frédéric Auguste (1834 Colmar, France - 1904 Paris) the perpetrator of the Lady of the Harbor, a.k.a. the Statue of Liberty, 63

Basler, Adolphe (1876 Poland - 1951) now forgotten Polish writer on modern art who spent 20 years in Montparnasse, but did not quite get it and sadly soured on it, but nonetheless wrote a number of indispensable works on it, 12

Bastien-Lepage, Jules (1848 Damvilliers, France - 1884 Paris) a painter who took the established Salon techniques and styles out into the open air and, thus, attempted to resolve the conflict between the Impressionists and the older generation; not everyone shared the elder Pissarro's opinion of his work: at his untimely death Jules Breton wrote that "France has lost her Holbein," 90

Baudelaire, Charles (1821 Paris - 1867 Paris) decadent poet whose volume *Les Fleurs du mal* (1857) was tried for obscenity; introduced Edgar Allan Poe to the French, 63

Beach, Sylvia (1887 Baltimore, Maryland - 1962 Paris) bookstore and lending library owner, daring and resourceful publisher in Paris (see also Monnier, Adrienne), 106, 119

Beauvoir, Simone de (1908 Paris - 1986 Paris) writer and sometime lover of Nelson Algren, a non-mainstream author who wrote about the wild side of life in Chicago, 18, 63

Beckett, Samuel (1906 Stillorgan, Dublin - 1989 Paris) an Irish writer who wrote much of his work in French; almost affianced to Joyce's unfortunate daughter, Lucia; joined the Resistance, for which the French awarded him two medals, and spent most of the war in hiding and in a serious depression in the South of France; lived most of his life in Paris, 104, 109

Benét, Stephen Vincent (1898 Bethlehem, Pennsylvania - 1943 New York City) writer of such messageladen works as *John Brown's Body* and *The Devil and Daniel Webster*, and the radio play, "They Burned the Books," performed on the NBC network in 1943 on the 10th anniversary of the nazi book burnings in Germany, 4

Bernhardt, Sarah (née Henriette Rosine Bernhard 1845 Paris - 1923 Paris) the greatest French actress of the modern acoustic theater, 120

Bing, Henri German art dealer in Paris before 1914, who clearly went out of his way to help his artists, allowing, for instance, Jules Pascin to stay at his apartment on Rue Lauriston; in 1907, Bing, having been introduced to Hermine David by Rudolf Levy, asked her to bring some of her work to his apartment to see if he might represent her, Pascin opened the door dressed in a kimono, the corset into which her mother had sewn Hermine did not long deter the two, who later married, 10

Bing, Siegfried (1838 Hamburg, Germany - ?) owner of the Salon de l'Art Nouveau and the art dealer responsible for bringing that style to the attention of the rather inattentive French, who seemed not to appreciate it except for subway entrance decoration, although certain French painters fell under its influence and created what we know as art nouveau; a naturalized French citizen, his gallery at 22, rue de Provence on the corner of Rue Chauchat also introduced Japanese art to Van Gogh and others, 55

Bistrot du Dôme a less elegant, less expensive cousin of the Café du Dôme, 15

Black Maria see **Panier à salade**

Blade Runner (1982) a cinematic vision of a robotic but filthy future in which the hero drives an undistinguished motor car around a movie lot, 61

Blanche, Jacques-Émile (1861 Paris - 1942 Auteuil, France) a wealthy society painter who wrote a generous amount of memoirs; known for his portraits, 90, 100

Bookstores, 34

Bondy, Walter (1883 Budapest - 1940 Toulon, France) Hungarian painter, despite his name; his father, Otto, moved the family to Vienna shortly after Walter's birth (Otto is perhaps meant by the reference to "the Czech Jew Oscar Bondy" whose art collection the nazis stole, in Lynn Nicholas', *The Rape of Europa. The Fate of Europe's Treasures in the Third Reich* [New York, 1994], a fascinating book); lived at 205 bis, Boulevard Raspail in 1910 and 3, rue Schoelcher in 1912, two doors from number 5 into which Picasso moved the next year remaining until 1916, which may not appear to be very exciting, but think of the times, then visit the locales! committed suicide by ceasing to take the insulin his severe diabetes required, rather than let the German and French nazi swine take him, 10

Bongard, Germaine designed clothes, operated her own dress-making shop, in which she held exhibitions, organized by her lover, Amédée Ozenfant, during the 1914-18 chapter of The Great Twentieth Century Sado-Masochism, the first of which she opened in December 1915 showing Léger, Matisse, Picasso, Kisling and Modigliani; after the battles temporarily ceased she opened the Gallery Thomas in her house in the Rue de Penthièvre (8th); one wonders what became of her, 40

Bonheur, Rosa (1822 Bordeaux, France - 1899 Château de By, Fontainebleau, France) a painter who admired the painter Stubbs; crossdressed for comfort and security; first woman elevated to the rank of officer in the Légion d'Honneur, 28

Bonnard, Pierre (1867 Fontenay-aux-Roses, France - 1947 Le Cannet, France) painter and illustrator who gave up Paris for the lightness of the Midi sun, but continued to return to the city; one of Lynn-Marie's favorites, 90

Bonvin, François (1817 Vaugirard, France - 1887 Saint-Germain-en-Laye, France) a painter who no doubt liked fine wine and who studied at the Académie Suisse (apparently misidentified by Milner as "Louis"), 28

Bouguereau, William-Adolphe (1825 La Rochelle, France - 1905 La Rochelle, France) a very successful genre painter, who taught at the Académie Julian and lost money each time he micturated, 28

Bourbon Restoration the temporary return of the not quite Ancien Régime, 23, 29

Bourdelle, Antoine Émile (1861 Montauban, France - 1929 Le Vésinet, France) sculptor with his own street in Paris, 5, 7, 51, 59-60

Bowen, Stella (1895 Adelaide, Australia - 1947 London?) a fine, if uninspired artist; for many years the life companion of Ford Madox Ford, life with whom she did not always enjoy but did not want to do without, though in the end she did; she contributed much, emotionally and materially, to Ford and others; spent many years in Paris during the roaring era, when she and Fordy partied with the best and the not so best, and in Provence with and without her companion; wrote about her life in *Drawn from*

Life (1940, Virago edition 1984), 41

Brancusi, Constantine (1876 Pestisani, Romania - 1957 Paris) sculptor and photographer in the modern but graceful style, whose name is invariably mispronounced by non-Romanians; his "Boy's Head" evokes memories of Augusta Savage's "Gamin," an interesting speculation on a previously unknown influence, if true in either direction, 63, 119, 121

Braque, Georges (1882 Argenteuil, France - 1963 Paris) a gentleman who actually got on well with the volatile Spaniard, Picasso, for several crucial years during which time they created cubism; Picasso never forgave him for being so talented, 91, 132

Brassaï (né Gyula Halasz, 1899 Brasso, Transylvania - 1984 Nice, France) a great walker of Paris nightbeat streets accompanied by his camera and certain friends, 778, 103

Bréa, Rue one of the shorter Paris streets both in name and length, 2

Breton, André (1896 Tinchebray-sur-Orne - 1966 Paris) the pope of surrealism, 25, 123, 127

Breton, Jules Adolphe Aimé Louis (1827 Courrières près d'Arras - 1906 Paris) a painter who believed with apparent sincerity that marriage and a family were dangerous to all concerned when one of the partners was an artist; author of *The Life of an Artist* (London, 1891), 28, 94

Brunelleschi, Umberto the only information one has on this person is in the text, except that he published an article entitled "Rosalie, l'hostessa di Modigliani" in *L'Illustrazione Italiana* (September 12, 1932), thus reducing Madame Rosalie to an appendage of the besotted artist, which she certainly was not (see entry for Chez Rosalie), 41

Café de Versailles on the Place de Rennes (now Place du 18 Juin 1940) across from the Gare Montparnasse, opened in 1869 with billiard tables and a bar, no longer extant; Scandinavian and French painters discovered it in the late 1890s; Stuart Merrill took Paul Fort there in 1901 to meet Edvard Diriks and Christian Krohg; Per Krohg practically grew up in the place where his father had a regular table for many years where his family drank and conversed with others including Oda's current lovers; by the late 1920s a dance-floor had been added, changing the milieu of the place, 104, 134

Café du Dôme a fine place to warm yourself and read the morning papers; also the locale where, between Christmas and New Year's Day 1907-08, an international conspiracy of Jews and foreigners met to plan the organizing and opening of the Académie Matisse, 8-16, 23, 66, 80, 92, 110, 123

Caillebotte, Gustave (1848 Paris - 1894 Gennevilliers, France) painter at one time known for his donation of Impressionist paintings to the French State, but now known for his large paintings of a rainy intersection (in the Chicago Art Institute), currently (1994-1995) undergoing a revival with major retrospectives in Paris and Chicago, 121

Calder, Alexander (1898 Philadelphia - 1976 New York City) a far too well-known American creator of monolithic, cute and colorful iron sculptures, 6, 131

Calvino, Italo (1923 Cuba - 1985 Rome) a writer of exquisite sentences of metaphysical and moral weight, but whose stories are also very funny on occasion, especially when the translation is good if one cannot read the original Italian, 89

Campagne-Première, Rue a street of studios, rooms, and apartments full of various talents, 35-41, 44, 53, 92

Capretz, Pierre linguist and creator of *French in Action*; possesses a fine taste for wine, 4

Carolus-Duran, Émile-Auguste (properly Charles-Auguste-Émile Durand 1837 Lille, France - 1917 Paris) formerly well-known French painter with too many dashes in his name, 28, 29

Cassoulet a pungent, wildly flavorful, but heavy bean and meat hot dish- from southwestern France, 18

Centre Georges Pompidou an architectural perversity (see also Musée National d'Art Moderne), 54, 61

Cézanne, Paul (1839 Aix-en-Provence - 1906 Aix-en-Provence) the originator of 20th century modern painting who hated Paris and loved rural Provence, 53, 101, 134

Chagall, Marc (né Moyshe Shagal 1887 Vitebsk, Russia - 1985 Saint-Paul-de-Vence, France) if you like floating fidlers and the color blue, you'll like this painter, 12

Chamberlin, Dean (b. 1949 Hempstead, New York) author's brother, a good companion in Paris, or elsewhere, but a severe literary critic, 70-71

Chambers, Robert W. (1865 Brooklyn, New York - 1933 New York City) prolific and forgotten American writer-illustrator enraptured with Paris before The Turn of the Century, 30

Chapu, Henri (1833 - 1891 Paris) yet another sculptor for a while en mode with a studio on the Rue Nôtre-Dame-des-Champs; commissioned to create a memorial to Balzac, fortunately he died before he could implement his maquette, 28

Chez Rosalie a small, but pungent, and lively beanery once upon a time on the Rue Campagne-Première; one of the multitudinous Parisian answers to the question "With all that hotel living, where did all these people eat?"; legend has it that Modigliani drank and supped here with Italian stone-cutters when he had no money because Rosalie felt sorry for him and presented no invoice at the end of the meal, 40, 97

Chicago Tribune **(Paris Edition)** newspaper now known only to academics who write about writers writing in Paris during the 1920s and 1930s, 13-14

Cimetière de Montparnasse an interesting place to visit, but..., 63, 65

Clark, Walter Van Tilberg (1909 Oreland, Maine - 1971 Reno, Nevada) an unfortunately forgotten American writer of classic stories of the American frontier and growing up in the western regions of the USA, 74

Classicism the hegemonic school rebelled against by the Romantics, 29

Claudel, Camille (1864 Villeneuve-sur-Fère, Aisne, France - 1943 Montfavet, Vaucluse, France) brilliant sculptor, unfortunate woman, 28, 31, 33

Closerie des Lilas formerly a good place for those without much dough to have a drink and meet people to heatedly discuss the latest; now a high-priced beanery, 23, 25, 79, 108

Cocteau, Jean (1889 Maisons-Lafitte, France - 1963 Paris) protean cultural personality whose incessant dabbling produced several lasting works in several media; has a museum in Menton on the Mediterranean Sea near the Italian border, which is worth a visit if you are near the town, and his color drawings decorate the Menton town hall marriage room, not really worth a visit unless you are already in town, 104, 122, 127

Comédie-Française, Le Théâtre de la the scene of many a scene after its founding in 1681, 29

Cottet, Charles (1863 Le Puy, Haute-Loire, France - 1925 Paris) a painter inspired by Gauguin and Puvis de Chavannes; painted mainly in Brittany; Jacques-Émile Blanche painted his portrait, 28

Coupole, La a popular and famous railroad waiting-room style restaurant, which still has dancing, 17-20, 114

Craig, Edward Henry Gordon (1872 Harpenden, England - 1966 Vence, France) the son of Ellen Terry and Edward Godwin who founded a theatrical school at the Arena Goldoni in Florence, Italy, and whose theater archives Hitler wanted for his own, and who is alleged to once have said, "The thing I want most at present is a complete collection of the records by Ethel Waters," which, since he allegedly said this in the late 1920s, shows a prescient appreciation for an unfortunately forgotten, marvellously inventive voice, 53

Croque-monsieur an extraordinarily rich melted ham and cheese sandwich, not for those on a low-fat diet, but when well made one of the culinary wonders of the civilized world, 16

Crosby, Caresse (1892 New York City - 1970 Rome) sometime publisher and owner of The Black Sun Press with her husband, Harry (1898 Boston, Massachusetts - 1929 New York City), who ran off with a younger woman whom he shot in the head before shooting himself in a mid-town Manhattan hotel room; author of an unreliable memoir of the period, 6

Cullen, Countée (1903 New York City - 1946 New York City) American Negro poet who wrote about black life in America, whose books include *The Ballad of the Brown Girl* and *The Black Christ*; when in Paris he hung out with a group which included Hale Woodruff and Palmer Hayden, whose Paris social headquarters was Augusta Savage's studio, 43, 57-58

Cunard, Nancy (1896 Leicestershire - 1965 Paris) owner of The Hours Press, publisher of the anthology *Negro* (1934), wearer of large baubles; died an unnecessarily lonely death, 43

Dadism a movement, 12, 25, 127, 129

Dardel, Nils (1888 Bettna, Sweden - 1943 New York City) after studying at the Stockholm academy in 1909-10, moved to Paris where he fell under the influence of Matisse, Cézanne, the Japanese and the naive painters (whether sequentially or simultaneously is not clear from the sources), 101

Dardel, Thora (née Klinkowström 1899 Djursholm, Sweden - ?) Swedish sometime sculpture student at the Académie Colarossi who posed for one of Modigliani's last paintings and married for the first time to the Swedish painter Nils Dardel, and worked as a journalist in Paris for Swedish newspapers and magazines during the 1920s,. 5

David, Hermine (1886 Paris - 1971 Paris?) student at the A c a d é m i e Julian; painter with a great deal of patience; longterm lover, wife and widow of Jules Pascin, 11, 123

Davidson, Jo (1883 New York City - 1952 Bercheron, France) American sculptor and memoirist who had to demolish his largest work for the usual reason, 13, 59

Défense, La example of inhuman fascist architecture which would have pleased Benito Mussolini, 61

Delambre, Rue a street mentioned in every Paris memoir which mentions Duff Twysden (a.k.a. Brett Ashley), 2, 15

Delaney, Beauford (1902 Nashville, Tennessee - 1977 Paris) a painter deserving of more attention than he has received thus far, though Henry Miller wrote an essay about him, 46

Depardieu, Gérard (b. 1948 Châteauroux) ubiquitous actor currently en mode, 33

Derain, André (1880 Chaton, France - 1954 Garches, France) consid-

ered by some in the late 1920s to be one of the main practition-
ers of "the French tradition" in painting, no doubt a chauvinist
reaction to the work of certain Jewish colleagues from Eastern
Europe and beyond, 90

Dickens, Charles (1812 Portsmouth, England - 1870 Godshill,
England) English writer who really does not belong here, but is,
8

Dingo Bar where Fitzgerald probably did not meet Hemingway, 2, 108

Diriks, Anna Maria (née Westerberg 1870 Uppsala, Sweden - 1932
Drobak, Norway) a Swedish artist usually referred to as Karl
Edvard's wife but with her own entry in the *Norsk Kunstner
Leksikon* (Oslo: Universitetsforlaget, 1982); lived in Paris for
two decades (1899 - 1921), during which time one hopes she
enjoyed herself beyond words, 5, 40, 105

Diriks, Karl Edvard (1855 Oslo - 1930 Horten, Norway) Norwegian
painter; husband of Anna; lived for 20 years (1899 to 1921) at
18, rue Boissonade near the Closerie des Lilas, where Paul Fort
edited the first issues of the journal *Vers et Prose*, 5, 40

Dodge, Mabel see Luhan, Mable Dodge

Dominique restaurant with Russian cuisine and Paris decor, 2, 4

Dos Passos, John Roderigo (1896 Unknown - 1970 Baltimore,
Maryland) American novelist who exemplified the questionable
notion that anyone who is not a socialist when young is inhu-
mane and anyone who is not a conservative when older is stupid,
74

Dreyfus, Alfred (1859 Mulhouse, France - 1935 Paris) a soldier who
only wanted to serve what he thought was his country, not
become a cause célèbre in the labyrinth of French nationalism
and antisemitism, 63

DuBois, William Edward Burghardt (1868 Barrington, Massachusetts
- 1963 Accra, Ghana) Negro intellectual, scholar, Communist
and pioneering civil rights activist, 46, 49, 58

Duchamp, Henri-Robert-Marcel (1887 Blainville, France - 1968
Neuilly-sur-Seine, France) Rrose Sélavy when in drag, 28, 37,
39, 119

Du Maurier, George Louis Palmella Busson (1834 Paris - 1896 London?) progenitor of Eliza Doolittle and Henry Higgens, sort of; definitely grandfather of Daphne du Maurier, 28

Dumas, Alexandre, dit père (1802 Villers-Cotterets, France - 1870 Puys, France) successful writer of potboilers, 28

Duncan, Raymond sometime manager of Pablo Casals' concerts; vegetarian; an urban William Morris who nonetheless possessed a strong desire to be a business executive; purveyor of hand-made leather sandals in Paris and environs; lived in the Rue de Seine during the 1930s where he hosted meetings of exiled anti-fascist intellectuals and writers, 42

Dunning, Ralph Cheever (1878 Detroit, Michigan - 1930 Paris) student of debilitation and sometime poet and protégé of Ezra Pound; apparently lived on no financial income and about whom not much is known, except that he seems to have died because he did not particularly like to eat, but did like his opium, and writing poems in distinctly "un-modern" idioms, which endeared him to the fragmented mind of the same Ezra Pound; rarely talked to anyone but Pound, Samuel Putnam and a few others; lived in "virtually a wooden box" (Wambly Bald) with only a cot, a stove, a bookcase and a straight-backed chair, 26

Durrell, Lawrence George (1912 Jullundur, India - 1990 Sommières, France) an extreme example of the myopia of the Nobel Prize Literature Committee, 18, 64, 93, 123

École des Beaux-Arts the art school with the wildest annual balls, 55, 57, 89

Ehrenburg, Ilya Grigoryevitch (1891 Kiev, Ukraine - 1967 Moscow) sometime Bolshevik Russian writer and publicist, one of the few prominent Jews who lived through the Stalin era to die of natural causes, 8-9

Eluard, Nusch (née Marie Benz, 1906 Germany - 1946 France) muse to her husband, Brassaï, Picasso, and Man Ray; photocollagist in the mid-1930s, 104

Eluard, Paul (né Eugène-Emile-Paul Grindel, 1895 Saint-Denis, France - 1952 Charenton, Paris) first husband of Gala Dali, only husband of the lovely Nusch and, after Nusch's death, of Dominique; member of the Resistance; according to one source, he authored a poem praising Stalin when he should have known better; subject of a fascinating exhibition at the Centre Georges Pompidou entitled *Eluard et ses amis peintres* (1982), 25

Emergency Rescue Committee established by prominent European refugees and concerned Americans to assist intellectuals, artists and scientists on the Gestapo wanted lists to get out of Europe; saved hundreds of them, 105

Ernani opera (1844) by G. Verdi, 30

Ernst, Max (1891 Brühl, Germany - 1976 Paris) part-time chess player, saved from the Gestapo's clutches by Peggy Guggenheim and Varian Fry, 25

Famous 1916 Photography Session, The on August 12, 1916, Jean Cocteau just happened to have his mother's camera filled with film in his bag when he met Picasso for lunch at the Carrefour Vavin; Picasso brought a number of friends with him and others showed up; the results can be seen in Billy Klüver's *Un jour avec Picasso. Le 12 août 1916* (Paris, 1994), 122

Fargue, Léon-Paul (1876 Paris - 1947 Paris) the ultimate Parisian pedestrian; author of *Le Piéton de Paris*, 63

Fidler, Eugène (1910 Balti, then Russian Empire, now Moldova - 1990 Roussillon, France) an artist of many talents whose work should be in more museums than it is; member of the Resistance in the South of France, he went into hiding in Roussillon where Samuel Beckett taught him English and where he remained after the war; his studio in that village provided a meeting place for all kinds of interesting people from the 1960s until his death, a tradition carried on by his wife, Edith, and daughter, Natacha, both ceramicists of high talent and ingenuity, 09

Fitch, Noël Riley author of the best book on Sylvia Beach, 14, 18

Fitzgerald, Francis Scott Key (1896 Saint Paul, Minnesota - 1940 Hollywood, California) American writer who did not believe in second acts for his countrymen, 14, 74, 102

Flanner, Janet (a.k.a. Genêt) (1892 Indianapolis, Indiana - 1978 New

York City) American writer who discovered a method of making a living by writing about the city while living in it, a circumstance some of us have yet to achieve, 51

Flechtheim, Alfred (1878 Münster, Germany - 1937 London) German art dealer, publisher of *Der Querschnitt*, and boxing fan, 10-11

Fondation Maeght a museum of modern art in Saint-Paul-de-Vence, well worth a visit, 7

Ford, Ford Madox (né Ford Hermann Hueffer, 1873 Merton, Surrey - 1939 Deauville, France) English writer, suffered from overproduction and suffers from under-appreciation, 26, 41

Fort, Paul (1872 Reims, France - 1960 Paris?) poet (indeed, at the death of Léon Dierx in 1912, those in charge of such things voted Fort into office as "prince des poètes"; one of the electors, Old Fred Mistral himself, noted after the election, "J'ai nommé Paul Fort, la cigale du Nord," which coming from Freddy was a high compliment); editor; friend of painters; lived at 24, rue Boissonade, a few doors from his friend, the tall Norwegian painter, Edvard Diriks; back issues of his journal crowded the apartment to the point where his family used them as tables and chairs; founder of the first Symbolist theater; author of the multitudinous *Ballades françaises*, 41, 97, 102, 118, 132

Frampton, Sir George James (1860 London - 1928 London?) English sculptor, possibly related to Peter, 28

Fry, Varian Mackey (1907 - 1967 Connecticut) with Lincoln Kirstein co-founded the literary magazine *Hound & Horn* in 1927, whilst both were undergraduates at Harvard, the title coming from an early Ezra Pound poem "The White Stag" ("Bid the world's hounds come to horn!"); headed the Emergency Rescue Committee's office in Marseilles 1940-1941, 104

Fuller, Meta Vaux Warrick (1877 Philadelphia, Pennsylvania - 1968 Framingham, Massachusetts) American Negro sculptor of powerful images who also studied with Rodin, 55-56

Garlic sausages a staple in every right-thinking household, 30

Gauguin, Eugène Henri Paul (1848 Paris - 1903 Atuana, Marquesas Islands) main character under a different name in Willy

Maugham's racy exposé of the world of modern art called *The Moon and Sixpence* (1919), 4-5

Gautier, Théophile (1811 Tarbes, France - 1872 Neuilly-sur-Seine) writer of macabre and morbid but almost perfectly formed poetry; exponent of the l'art pour l'art doctrine, 29

Germans in Paris, 10-12, 21, 54, 68-69, 76, 92

Gerassi, John author of an idiosyncratic biographical study of Jean-Paul Sartre, 18

Gérome, Jean-Léon (1824 Vesoul, France - 1904 Paris) painter, owner of the monkey Jacques; vehement opponent of the Impressionists' work, 26, 28

Giacometti, Alberto (1901 Borgonovo near Stampa, Switzerland - 1966 Chur, Switzerland) sculptor, 7, 76, 118

Gide, André (1869 Paris - 1951 Paris) a complex man of literature, one of the few to achieve the top level of European culture with his works and his life, the latter of which was relatively open in its bisexuality; never really played the role of Grand Old Man of French Letters, but could have; instead kept up with what was new through friendships with people such as Adrienne Monnier, Sylvia Beach, Klaus Mann, and Roger Martin du Gard, 117, 121

Goetz, Richard German painter who came to Paris in 1900 and moved into Whistler's studio at 86, rue Nôtre-Dame-des-Champs in 1901; showed at the Salon des Indépendants; left Paris in August 1914, but returned after 1919, this time as a collector of French art no longer himself interested in painting; before 1911 in his Rue du Cardinal Lemoine apartment occasionally served roast geese to the artists who hacked at it "with saws and hatchets," according to Fernande Olivier; became a naturalized citizen of the USA at some point in his life, 10

Goldfarb, Shirley (1925 Altoona, Pennsylvania - 1980 Paris) American painter who lived most of her all too brief adult life in Paris; author of the posthumously published *Carnets. Montparnasse 1971-1980* (Paris: Quai Voltaire, 1994), 63

Gottlieb, Léopold (1883 Drohobycz, Poland - 1934 Paris) an artist whose sensitivities resulted in an early morning duel with his colleague, Kisling; unknown today, but André Salmon published a book about him in 1927, 40, 83, 112

Grande Chaumière, Rue de la home of the art school, decades of intrigues, and waiting models, 4-5, 31, 53

Green, Julien (b. 1900 Paris) American-French writer and diarist still madly in love with the city at 96 years of life, 60-61

Greenwich Village an area in downtown Manhattan once upon a time a haven for artistically inclined folk with and without talent, 46

Grünewald, Isaac (1889 Stockholm - 1946 Sweden) Swedish artist; member of the Dôme circle before 1914, who earned some money as a good-luck charm for the poker players in the café; a student at the Académie Matisse after falling completely under the Frenchman's influence when the latter's radical use of color put a spell on the former upon his arrival in Paris in 1908; lived in poverty for several years, dancing all night to keep warm and sleeping on the billiard tables in the Café de Versailles for a few hours before hurrying off to the Matisse school; his cheap hotel room had no functioning heating system; drank occasionally with Per Krohg and Pascin, who painted his portrait; left France in 1911 to work at the Stockholm Opera; when he returned to Paris in 1921 he moved into the top floor studio at 86, rue Nôtre-Dame-des-Champs; taught from 1932-1942 at Stockholm Art Academy; died in an airplane accident, 107

Guggenheim, Peggy (née Marguerite 1898 New York City - 1979 Venice, Italy) a rare personage, who did much to make our lives more enjoyable, often through cold-blooded wheeler-dealing in the cut-throat art dealer world, 104

Guide Michelin a red bible of sorts, 15, 23

Hamnett, Nina (1890 Tenby, South Wales - 1956 London) English painter and writer about whom many stories of outlandish behavior are told, who would eagerly disrobe and dance in sketching class if asked, because she knew she had a very displayable body; not without reason did she entitle her memoirs *Laughing Torso* (New York: Ray Long and Richard R. Smith, 1932), must reading; lived for some time at 8, rue de la Grande

Chaumière with Zawado; memorized a large repertoire of bawdy songs, such as "Bollocky Bill the Sailor" and "She Was Honest But She Was Poor," which she often sang at Pizzuti's Italian restaurant across the street from the Dingo Bar; according to one source she liked sailors a lot, occasionally even large groups of them, but this is tawdry phallocentric gossip from an era before "political correctness" began its reign of censorship; reputed to have a fine drawing hand which resulted in many direct and meticulous paintings; fell or threw herself out of her apartment window whilst drunk and died; there is, of course, much more to be said about her, but in another place, 4, 132, 134

Hansen, Arlen (b. 1936)   author of an entertaining and useful book, containing only a few inaccuracies, entitled *Expatriate Paris: A Cultural and Literary Guide to Paris of the 1920s* (New York: Arcade Publishing, 1990), 37, 40, 62

Harlem Renaissance   a misnomer for a not very exact period of time during which American Negro artists and writers, many of whom lived or worked in Harlem, flourished, 56

Harrison, Alexander (1853 Philadelphia, Pennsylvania - 1930 Paris) American painter known in his last years during the 1920s as The Grand Old Man of Montparnasse who studied and worked in Paris during the late 19th century and into the 20th, when, at the end of his life, almost 80, he sipped his night-cap with the younger crowd at the Closerie des Lilas before returning to his Rue Val-de-Grâce studio; painted the pastoral nudes in a curious arbor entitled "En Arcadie," and at one point all the European capitals knew his work; one of the first plein air painters to move his nude models out of the studio into the open countryside, 26

Hartley, Marsden (1877 Lewiston, Maine - 1943 Corea, Maine) American painter with a taste for laborers' clothing; Gertrude Stein put him in a play; in the end a difficult man to know, 61f

Hawks, Howard (1896 Goshen, Indiana - 1977 Palm Springs, California)   an adventurer who found work in Hollywood, 17

Hayden, Henri (1883 Warsaw - 1970 Paris) arrived in Paris in 1907, but lived in relative isolation until 1914 when he moved to Montparnasse; worked with Erik Satie and Les Six; became a French citizen in the early 1920s; fled Paris to the South of France in June 1942 hiding in the Auvergne, Mougins, and finally in the perched village of Roussillon (Vaucluse), where he met the ceramicist and collagist Eugène Fidler, also in hiding from the Gestapo, as was Samuel Beckett; returned to Paris in the Autumn of 1944, he discovered his studio and works he'd left there destroyed, so he began again, 38, 127

Hayden, Palmer (1890 Widewater, Virginia - 1973 New York City) American Negro painter who lived in Paris, 44, 127

Hayter, Stanley William (1901 Hackney, London - 1988 Paris) etcher who worked for the Anglo-Iranian Oil Company 1922-25, after which he survived Surrealism to become one of the great innovative printmakers of his day; ran his own printmaking school, named Atelier 17, at 17, rue Campagne-Première 1933-39, after which he moved to New York City to escape the Huns, 40, 53, 101

Hébuterne, Jeanne (1898 Paris - 1920 Paris) art student; lovely, but unfortunate lover of Modigliani and mother of his children: leapt to her death from the top floor of her nasty parents' apartment building at 8 bis, rue Amyot behind the Panthéon a day and a half after the artist died, 4-5, 119

Heggen, Thomas (1919 Fort Dodge, Iowa - 1949 New York City) short-lived author of *Mr. Roberts*, one of the finest novels about Americans in the Pacific theater during the 1941-45 Era of Mass Stupidity, 73

Hemingway, Ernest Miller (1899 Oak Park, Illinois - 1961 Ketchum, Idaho) began the trend of fictionalized memoirs with *A Moveable Feast*, published shortly after his suicide, which must nonetheless be read by anyone fascinated by Paris, *passim*

***Hernani* Battle, The Famous** (1830) cause of Victor Hugo losing his lease in the Rue Nôtre-Dame-des-Champs, 29-30

Hiler, Hilaire played the piano accompaniment to Kiki's boisterous

Jacob, Max (1876 Quimper, France - 1944 Drancy transit camp, Paris) gentle poet whose conversion to Roman Catholicism many years before did not save him from the nazi swines' definition of a Jew, 91, 122

Jacques pet monkey who sat at table in a formal white cravat with the guests unless he misbehaved, in which case he was banned until he put on a rag-picker's rags, then he could return to the meal, suitably chastened, one supposes, 28, 106

James, Henry (1843 New York City - 1916 London) one of the last grand American novelists with big themes and something to say to all of us, 69, 73

Jardin du Luxembourg (also known as the Luxembourg Garden) one of Paris' pigeon hunting areas for poor struggling hungry writers and their families, 54, 73

Jockey, Le (1923-1930) at 146, boulevard du Montparnasse, a spiffy nightclub at the Rue Campagne-Première corner managed and decorated in a mock cowboy and Indian motif by the American cultural polymath Hilaire Hiler; patronized by both American and French writers, artists, and hangers-on, including Kiki who sang filthy songs and danced there; according to McAlmon "almost anybody of the writing, painting, musical, gigoloing, whoring, pimping or drinking world was apt to turn up at the Jockey"; not to be confused with the Jockey Club, home-away-from-home of the rich and aristocratic French, 35, 109, 120

Johnson, William Henry (1901 Florence, South Carolina - 1970 Central Islip, New York) American Negro painter who lived in France and Denmark, 44

Jolas, Eugene (1894 Union-Hill, New Jersey - 1952 Paris) proponent of the "Revolution of the Word" and literary assistant to James Joyce; author of the unpublished autobiography *Man from Babel*, which one would like to read if one knew where it is located, 13

Jones, Lois Mailou (b. 1905 Boston, Massachusetts) American Negro painter who studied in France and returned many times there and to Haiti to recharge her creative energies, 44

Joyce, James Augustine Aloysius (1882 Rathgar, Dublin - 1941 Zürich, Switzerland) a Dublin writer who wrote only about Dublin while living all his adult life on the Continent, 13, 74, 94, 111, 118, 131f.

Joyce, Lucia (1907 Trieste, Italy - 1982 Northampton, England) a possibly brilliant woman whose father rather believed her clairvoyant than demented; her life cannot even be imagined, 94

Julian, Rodolphe (1839 La Palud, Vaucluse, France - 1907 Paris) painter and art teacher; founder of the Académie Julian and its many branches throughout the city, all of which brought him wealth if not taste, 89

Jungle, The (1927 - ca. 1937) a sort of dance-hall patronized by a spectrum of types ranging from ambiguous Surrealists to bourgeois housewives from the 16th arrondissement and tourists looking for a quick jigjiggle thrill, 34f.

Kaelin, Martin director of the Académie Colarossi during the summer of 1915 when he refused to allow the continuation of the concerts, so successful the past Winter, for reasons still not clear to me, 40, 83

Kafka, Franz (1883 Prague - 1924 Kierling, Austria) wrote exemplary modernist fiction, but never heard Lee Konitz play, 61

Kickert, Conrad (1882 The Hague - 1965 Paris) Netherlandish artist who could not follow the cubist path; had a studio near the Montparnasse railroad station which he kindly gave to Mondrian, the place now obliterated by human greed and indifference; lived for much of his life in Paris beginning in 1909, whereafter he inhabited 33, avenue du Maine (1912), 26, rue du Départ, 18 rue Boissonade (1925-36) and 33, rue Boissonade (1937-65), 40, 62

Kiki de Montparnasse (née Alice Ernestine Prin 1901 Châtillon-sur-Seine, France - 1953 Paris) a well-known serious person with extraordinary pizzazz, 6, 36, 38, 111, 115, 117, 131

Kisling, Moïse (1891 Krakow, Poland - 1953 Sanary-sur-mer, France) a painter about whom many stories are told, most of them true, such as his early morning duel in the Parc des Princes on June

12, 1914, with his countryman, Léopold Gottlieb, concerning an unidentified "question of honor," after which both claimed victory since each cut the other with cavalry sabers during the heated exchange of The Old Thrust and Parry, 36, 96, 107, 122, 134

Klément, Rudolph (1910 Hamburg, Germany - 1938 Paris) unfortunate secretary to Leon Trotsky, 27

Klüver, Billy (b. 1927) co-author of a lavishly, indeed profusely, illustrated book about Montparnasse, 6, 9, 104, 114

Konitz, Lee (b. 1927 Chicago, Illinois) one of those figures the general public has never heard of, but without whose contribution today's music would sound much worse, as difficult as it may be to think such a thing possible, 112

Knudsen, Grethe (b. 1955 Tonder, Denmark) Danish artist and Paris resident, 21

Kramstyk, Roman (1885 - 1942 Lodz ghetto, Poland) Polish artist who lived in Paris for many years and was still there in 1925, which bit of information we know because he appears in the photograph of a group on the terrace of La Rotonde taken at the time; his painting "Deep in Thought" is in the Chicago Polish Museum, 113

Krohg, Christian (1852 Aker near Oslo - 1925 Oslo) broad-minded full-bearded patriarch and Norwegian painter and journalist; father of Per; second husband of Oda; moved back to Oslo from France in 1910 to become head of the new Academy of Fine Arts, 5, 97

Krohg, Lucy (née Cecile Vidil 1890 - ?) model, muse, mother, wife, mistress, magnetically sensual, and a great dancer of the tango, 5-6, 40, 83, 123, 131

Krohg, Oda (née Othilia Lasson 1860 Asgardstrand, Norway - 1935 Oslo) painter; free-spirited wife of Christian, mother of Per and other children, lover of a number of acquaintances and friends long before such a style of living became something other than utterly outrageous, 5, 98

Krohg, Per Lasson (1889 Asgardstrand, Norway - 1965 Oslo) painter; king of the Scandinavian tango; husband of Lucy and father of

Guy (b. 1917 Oslo), a painter; later husband of Ragnhild Helene Andersen and father of Morton (b. 1937 Oslo), also a painter, 5-6, 40, 83, 97, 107, 131

Kronenbourg a fine Alsatian beer, 16

Ladd, Alan (1913 Hot Springs, Arkansas - 1964 Palm Springs, California) portrayer of short cowboys and at least one assassin, 52

Lafon, René original owner of La Coupole, 19

Landshoff, Fritz (1901 Berlin - 1988 Amsterdam, Netherlands) editor and publisher; forced by the nazi regime into exile, he founded the German branch of the Querido publishing house in Amsterdam to publish writers who could no longer be printed in Germany, thus keeping many impoverished authors alive and their works in print; barely escaped to New York as the nazis and their collaborators shot out all the lights in Europe plunging the continent into a new dark age, 92

Laurens, Jean-Paul (1838 Fourquevaux, France - 1921 Paris) painter with a studio in the Rue Nôtre-Dame-des-Champs; painted the Théâtre de l'Odéon ceiling; taught among others Alphonse Mucha at the Académie Julian, 28

Le Fauconnier, Henri French painter; member of the loosely associated group often linked as "second generation cubists," most of whom had no idea what cubism meant; indeed, based on the one painting of his, of which I have seen a photograph, Le Fauconnier was no cubist at all (see Klüver and Martin, 47, "Mountain People Attacked by Bears"); lived at 19, rue Visconti (6th) 1905-10, whereafter he moved to the Rue Nôtre-Dame-des-Champs (where else?), 28

Léger, Fernand (1881 Argentan, France - 1955 Gif-sur-Yvette, France) tubist painter with a museum in Biot, 7, 26, 90, 119

Leiris, Michel (1901 Paris - 1990 Paris) a mystic Parisian anthropologist-poet and creator of aphorisms who played the role of Big Foot in Picasso's play, *Le Désir attrappé par la queue* (Desire Caught by the Tail) in its first reading under Albert Camus' direction in the occupation Paris Spring of 1944, one of those magical nights that no one believes happened the next day, 25

Lenin, V.I. (né Vladimir Ilych Ulyanov 1870 Simbirsk, Russia - 1924 Gorki, Russia) according to some a close competitor with A. Hitler for the title of font of 20th century evil, but also a habitué of cafés and bars, 9

Levy, Julien as a young man was lucky enough to marry Joelle, daughter of Mina Loy; owned an art gallery in New York and Paris where he knew everybody; wrote a book about it all entitled *Memoir of an Art Gallery* (1977), in 1927 he first saw Atget's photographs in Man Ray's studio in the Rue Campagne-Première and began to buy as many as the old photographer would sell; he assisted Berenice Abbott in saving the glass plates for posterity after Atget's death later that year; one of the few men who turned Kiki down, upon which incident she told him "Vous n'êtes pas un homme, mais un hommelette," 40

Levy, Rudolf (1875 Stettin, Pomerania, Germany - 1944 en route to Auschwitz) German painter who managed the Matisse Academy for a brief period; forced by the nazi regime out of Berlin in 1933 his life became a debilitating odyssey that wound its way through the South of France, Rapallo, to Mallorca until the civil war after which he went to the USA for a brief period, then in 1937 to the Yugoslav island of Sipanska Luka by Dubrovnik, whence he moved in early 1938 to Ischia, and finally to a form of hiding in Florence where he could occasionally sell a painting and where his former wife, the actress Genia Morelli in Munich, could send him money orders; exactly how the Gestapo found him is not clear to me, but the nazis infested Florence and his presence could not have been a very big secret, 4, 9, 94, 124

Lewis, Harry Sinclair (1885 Sauk Centre, Minnesota - 1951 Rome, Italy) renegade Minnesotan, 15

Lipchitz, Jacques (né Chaim-Jacob Lipchitz 1891 Druskieniki, Lithuania - 1973 Capri, Italy) sculptor who arrived in Paris in 1909; studied at the École-des-Beaux-Arts with Injalbert, the Académie Colarossi and the Académie Julian; became a French citizen in 1924; forced to flee the nazis in 1940-41; spent the war years in the USA, 90

Lists 7, 26, 28, 36, 40-41

Lockridge, Ross Jr. (1914 Bloomington, Indiana - 1948 Bloomington, Indiana) another unfortunate American suicide, possibly unable to cope with success, 73f.

Lord, James (b. 1922 Englewood, New Jersey) biographer and gossipy memoirist, 7

Loren, Sophia (b, 1934 Rome, Italy) poster idol in the late 1960s, 52

Loy, Mina (1882 London - 1966) trained as a painter in Paris before 1914 when she had a studio at 17, rue Campagne-Première in 1905; married an English artist with whom she had the first of her two "raving beauty" daughters, the second of whom she had with her second husband, Arthur Craven, Oscar Wilde's nephew, in New York City shortly after which he disappeared into a desert and she returned to Paris, living with the girls at 9, rue Saint-Romain (6th), where she wrote poetry and made lampshades of her own design; author of *Lunar Baedecker* (1923), misspelled by her publisher, Robert McAlmon; published an interesting critical interpretation of Gertrude Stein's style in the *Transatlantic Review* (1924); appears as Patience Scalpel in the risqué *Ladies Almanack,* published anonymously in Paris (1928); her collected poetry was published as *The Last Lunar Baedeker* (1982); one of her more notable lines reads "Pig Cupid, his rosy snout rooting erotic garbage," which, according to William Carlos Williams, everyone remembered; her technical experimentation in style and feminist subject matter kept readers away in droves, alas, 40, 84, 115, 119

Luhan, Mable Dodge (1879 Buffalo, New York - 1962) a well-off hostess with a yen for writing memoirs about her life with artsy types throughout a good part of the 20th century; contributed to the popularity of Taos, New Mexico, 53

MacMonnies, Frederick William (1863 Brooklyn, New York - 1937 New York City) American sculptor of the late 19th century with a studio in Paris; the very handsome fellow also taught painting classes for women only in the mid-1890s at the Académie Vitti

(49, boulevard du Montparnasse), 50

Maillol, Aristide Joseph Bonaventure (1861 Banyuls-sur-Mer, France - 1944 Banyuls-sur-Mer, France) randy French sculptor who insulted his wife and liked the Germans too much, 59f.

Malet, Léo (1908 Montpellier, France -1996 Paris) poet, anarchist, creator of "found" art, and writer of detective novels, 27

Mann, Klaus (1906 Munich, Germany - 1949 Cannes, France) member of the German literary family who lived a complicated life, possessed a tremendous talent, spent a good deal of his short life working for the benefit of others, and killed himself; posthumously his books became well-known in reprint editions, including his memoirs, but not his book on André Gide, 91f

Marcuse, Herbert (1898 Berlin - 1979 Starnberg, Germany) a part-time socio-politologist in California for a long part of his life, 18

Martin, Julie co-author of the one big book on Montparnasse using Kiki as its centripetal force, 6, 9, 114

Masurovsky, Gregory (b. 1929 The Bronx, New York) American artist and teacher resident in Paris since 1954, 19, 21-22

Mathé, Sylvie linguist and professor in Provence with a fine taste for wine, 4

Matisse, Henri (1869 Le Cateau-Cambrésis, France - 1954 Nice, France) praised as one of the great painters of the 20th century by hoodwinked acolytes; ran an art school, the Matisse Academy, for a few years before 1914, 4, 6, 90, 96, 98, 107, 115, 124

Matisse, Pierre art gallery owner, 7

Matthiessen, Peter (b. 1927 New York City) risk-taking writer and co-founder of *The Paris Review*, 66

Maupassant, Henry-René-Albert-Guy de (1850 Château de Miromesnil près de Dieppe - 1893 Paris) one of the creators of the modern short story; a sufferer of constant arousal; *The Reader's Encyclopedia* (1948) notes that "as a result of overwork he became insane near the end of his life," but it was rather more complicated than that, 63

Mayakovsky, Vladimir (1893 Bagadadi, Georgia, Russian Empire - 1930, Moscow, Stalinist Empire) the most prominent Soviet poet who began his career as a Futurist; traveled to Paris in October 1924 hoping to obtain a tourist visa to the USA; Elsa Triolet, who knew him earlier in Moscow and Berlin, then living at the Hôtel Istria, got him a room there ("it's the cheapest and the cleanest"); his visa application denied, he returned to Moscow at the end of December, alas; remained a free-thinking spirit who really believed in the Revolution's promises, all of which (in addition to the usual destructive emotional entanglements of Russian poets) made his life intolerable where he lived, and he shot himself rather than continue to be disillusioned, 36

Mayo, Flora Lewis (1900 Denver, Colorado - ? California) art student, who came to Paris in 1925; at the age of 27, became passionate about and for a time influenced the style of her fellow student Alberto Giacometti, who, after five years, advised she return to the USA, which she did after, alas, destroying all her own work; according to James Lord, "she ended her days in demented solitude," 7

McAlmon, Robert (1896 Clifton,Kansas - 1956 Desert Hot Springs, California)) indirectly received a considerable sum of money from England's richest man, with which he subsidized Joyce and published younger writers in his Contact Editions, also writer of some good, if hasty short stories, 26, 37, 111, 116, 119

Mercader, Ramon (a.k.a. Frank Jacson 1914 - 1978 Havana, Cuba) Léon Trotsky's murderer, 27

Mérimée, Prosper (1803 Paris - 1870 Cannes, France) sometime inspector-general of historic monuments in France; writer of potboiler historical novels, 28

Merrill, Stuart Fitzgerald (1863 near Whitman's birthplace on Long Island, New York - 1915 Versailles, France) American poet who wrote mainly in French; member of the Symbolist journal *Vers et Prose* circle around Paul Fort and the Closerie des Lilas, when poets could afford to drink and eat there; disinherited by his father for supporting the Haymarket Riot defendants, he left the USA in 1892 in bitterness and never returned; nevertheless he helped subsidize several avant-garde journals such as *La Révolte* and the very influential *La Revue Blanche*; author of the frightening sentence "The Symbolist is the anarchist of literature," 97

Miller, Henry Valentine (1891 Brooklyn, New York - 1980 Los Angeles, California) the most American of Parisians, 18, 46, 64, 93, 101, 123

Mills, Mariette American sculptress; her husband Heyworth built and repaired model ships; friend of Satie, Duchamp, Brancusi, Picabia, Léger, Mina Loy, McAlmon (her bust of whom was shown in the Louvre in 1923), and many other writers and artists of various nationalities; their Montparnasse studio formed one of the social and artistic focal points during the Interregnum between the sessions of the Great 20th Century Dark Age, 40

Milner, John English author of a useful but irritatingly incomplete volume on Paris studios in the 19th century, 28, 96

Mistral, Frédéric (Frédéri) (1830 Mas du Juge prés de Saint-Remy de-Provence, France - 1914 Maillane, France) Nobel Prize winning poet and scholar who refused to believe that Provençal was a dead language or that Provençal culture only existed for the archeologists; established a museum in Arles for that culture's artifacts with his Nobel money, 105

Modigliani, Amedeo (1884 Livorno, Italy - 1920 Paris) painter of lengthy unshaven naked women; lover of Jeanne Hébuterne and others, 4, 40, 96, 99, 101, 109, 122

Mondrian, Piet (1872 Amersfoort, Netherlands - 1944 New York City) Netherlandish painter of hip squares, 62, 112

Monocle, Le famous lesbian bar near the hetero whorehouse Le Sphinx, both no longer extant per se, 78

Monnier, Adrienne (1892 Paris - 1954 Les Déserts, France) publisher and bookstore owner in Paris (see also Beach, Sylvia), 33, 94

Montdevergues asylum for the mentally deranged in Montfavet (Vaucluse), 33

Montparnasse, Boulevard du thoroughfare bisecting the mythological kingdom of Parnassus Mountain, 8, 16, 23, 31, 34

Montparnasse cemetery see Cimetière de Montparnasse

Montparnasse high-rise one of the travesties of the 20th century; see Louis Chevalier's book *The Assassination of Paris* (expanded English edition University of Chicago Press, 1994), in which the admirable author examines the whole despicable development of the attempt to destroy the city under the guise of "modernization," and Norma Evenson, *Paris: A Century of Change 1878-1978* (Yale University Press, 1979) for changes wrecked upon the cityscape and Parisians, 60-61

Moore, George (1852 Ballyglass, County Mayo, Ireland - 1933 London?) Irish journalist and novelist who spent his youth in Paris, wrote in French at the beginning of his prodigiously productive career and knew everybody one should have known; also studied "art" for a short while in Montparnasse, 89

Moreau-Vauthier, Auguste-Jean (1831 Paris - 1893 Paris) now forgotten, once fashionable doublenamed doublenamed ivory sculptor who did the oversized figure of La Parisienne for the monumental gate at the Exposition Universelle of 1900; his book on the painter Gérôme (1906) describes the bucolic cityscape of the Rue Nôtre-Dame-des-Champs around the year 1860: "...paths of beaten earth fringed with grass...," 28

"Mornard, Jacques" see Mercader, Ramon

Motley, Archibald John (1891 New Orleans, Louisiana - 1981 Chicago, Illinois?) American Negro painter who studied in Paris painting scenes of city life as he saw it, especially interiors of The Jockey and the Bal Nègre, 46

Mucha, Alphonse Marie (1860 Ivancice, Bohemia - 1938 Prague) creator of the art nouveau poster style who shared his first name with Al Capone; achieved fame if not fortune after Sarah Bernhardt "discovered" him in 1897; his poster of La Grande Sarah as Medea (1898) is still known today, 4, 114

Mühsam, Erich (1878 Berlin - 1934 Oranienburg concentration camp, Germany) German anarchist poet who felt comfortable in Paris and should have remained there; having survived being beaten almost to death, during his incarceration 1919-24 in the Niederschönenfeld prison in Bavaria for having participated in the Bavarian Soviet Republic, his fellow Germans later viciously tortured him in the Brandenburg penitentiary, whereafter they hanged him in the concentration camp; his wife Zenzi survived both the German and the Soviet camps, 10

Musée Bourdelle contains a lot of his work no one else apparently wanted, 59

Musée du Luxembourg once a comfy place to look at the Caillebotte Donation and other fine paintings, 42

Musée National d'Art Moderne located partially in the Centre Georges Pompidou, that epitome of ugliness, contains post-Post-Impressionist art, 43, 54

Musée d'Orsay locale of Impressionist and Post-Impressionist paintings and other artifacts jammed into niches and behind pillars of the old railroad station, items formerly in the Jeu de Paume and before that in the Musée du Luxembourg, 54

Nadelman, Elie (1882 Warsaw - 1946 Riverdale, Bronx, New York) came to Paris via Munich in 1904 to study at the Académie Colarossi; met Picasso in 1908 through Leo Stein; in 1911 Helena Rubinstein began to buy his work and in 1914 helped him to emigrate to the USA where he lived from then on, becoming a citizen in 1927, 40

Nerval, Gérard de (1808 Paris - 1855 Paris) the Romantic who did indeed walk his pet lobster on a rhinestone leash, 29f.

Ney, Michel de la Moskova, Prince (1769 Saarlouis, France - 1815 Paris) French general who supported Napoléon I at the cost of his life; much admired by Ernest Hemingway, 23

Nin, Anaïs (1903 Paris - 1977 Los Angeles, California) creator of a massive novel entitled *The Diaries of Anaïs Nin*, 6, 18

Noguchi, Isamu (1904 Los Angeles, California - 1988 New York City) American sculptor and designer of stage productions of some repute; studied with Brancusi in Paris France; designed the sculpture garden on the grounds of the Israel Museum of Art in Jerusalem and his own garden museum in Long Island City, New York, 7

Nourritures Terrestres, Les bookstore no doubt named after André

Gide's book of youthful poetry published in 1897, 34, 86

Nôtre-Dame-des-Champs, Rue a street dense with ghosts of a cultural past, 26-28, 30f, 42, 53

Olivier, Fernande (née Amilie Lang 1881 Paris - 1966 Paris) Picasso's first long-term female companion; possessed a certain talent for drawing and a remarkable memory; later wrote down everything; and convinced the painter to ensure she had no material need to publish the second volume of her *Souvenirs intimes*, which appeared anyway after the two protagonists died, 106

Ortis de Zarate, Manuel (1886 Como, Italy - 1946 Los Angeles, California or New York City) Chilean painter and art teacher who participated in The Famous Photography Session on August 12, 1916, at the Carrefour Vavin along with Jean Cocteau, Max Jacob, the model Pâquerette, André Salmon, Modigliani, Picasso, Henri-Pierre Roché, Marie Vassilieff, and Moïse Kisling, 4

Ozenfant, Amédée (1886 Saint-Quentin, France - 1966 Cannes) another of the second generation cubist painters; moved to Paris in 1905; hovered on the fringe of the dadaists' activities, but in 1917 developed the "Purist" school of painting which consisted of him and Charles-Edouard Jeanneret (Le Corbusier) demanding a totally rational approach to painting; edited art-ideological journals, wrote books on modern art; taught at the Académie Moderne and at his own studio-schools in London (1935-38) and New York City (1939-55), after which he returned to France, 40, 96

Pach, Walter (1883 -1958) American artist and writer; translator of Elie Faure's 5-volume *History of Art* and author of a book on Renoir and one entitled *Queer Thing, Painting* (1938), 40, 83

Pâquerette (née Emilienne Pâquerette Geslot) a fashion model for the famous Paul Poiret; met artists and writers in Montparnasse before, during and perhaps after the first chapter of The Great 20th Century Abattoir; one of Picasso's lovers 1916-1917; married Dr. Raymond Barrieu, Kisling's second in the famous 1914 duel, 122

Panier à salade see Black Maria

Paris Review, The a periodical, 14, 63f., 73

Pascin, Jules (né Julius Mordecai Pincas 1885 Vidin, Bulgaria - 1930 Paris) lover of Lucy Krohg and Hermine David; self-destructive painter of some repute, 4-5, 11, 94f., 101, 107, 131

Paul, Elliot Harold (1891 Malden, Massachusetts - 1958 Providence, Rhode Island) author of mystery novels in which the characters sit a lot in the Café du Dôme, 13-14

Perec, Georges (1936 Paris - 1982 Paris) author of a great many works the reading of which only deepens the mysteries, 88f.

Perlès, Alfred (1896 Vienna - 1990 Wells, England) writer known as Joey to his pals Henry Miller and Lawrence Durrell, 64, 93

Picabia, Francis Marie Martinez (1879 Paris - 1953 Paris) painter and writer; at one point just after 1918 (according to some) considered to be the big daddy of dadaists, as famous as Picasso; lover of expensive motor cars and fast women; publicly broke with the dadaists in May 1921 to protest their increasing ideological rigidity and Breton's ex cathedra behavior, thereafter painted in an eccentric style unique to himself; moved to Mougins, Provence in 1925; in the 1930s became friendly with Gertrude Stein; returned to Paris at the end of the Second Chapter of the Great 20th Century Suppuration and took to abstraction again, 36, 39, 119

Picasso, Pablo Ruiz (1881 Malaga, Spain - 1973 Mougins, France) Spanish painter considered French by the cognoscenti, 53, 93f., and *passim*

Pissarro, Camille (1830 St. Thomas, US Virgin Islands - 1903 Paris) an Impressionist painter with a mind so fine but flexible that pointillisme penetrated it, 90, 94

Pissarro, Lucien (1863 Paris - 1944 Heywood, Somerset, England) son of Camille; a fine engraver and woodcutter, 90

Plimpton, George (b. 1927 New York City) compiler of experiences for successful books, sometime supplier of banned schnapps, 14, 66ff.

Poe, Edgar Allan (1809 Boston, Massachusetts - 1849 Baltimore,

Maryland) American creator of the classic police procedural; sometime poet and substance abuser, 94

Poiret, Paul (1879 Paris - 1944 Paris) a very well-known designer of female clothing who dabbled in The Arts and designed camouflage patterns for the French army during the 1914-1918 chapter of The Period of Self-Delusion; not able to find a place for himself in his milieu after 1918; died in poverty, 40, 122

Pomeroy, Frederick William (1857 London - 1924 Clintonville) English sculptor, 28

Porter, Katherine Anne (1894 Indian Creek, Texas - 1980 Silver Spring, Maryland) author of the wonderfully titled book of stories *Pale Horse, Pale Rider* (1939) who left her papers to the University of Maryland, 26

Pound, Ezra Loomis (1885 Hailey, Idaho - 1972 Venice, Italy) one of the vital midwives of 20th century English language literature, a fine, if all too often obscure poet, an economic theory crank, and, alas, a suburban antisemite, 26, 51, 103, 105, 127, 129

Presley, Elvis an American pop cultural phenomenon who could actually sing the blues quite effectively in his youth, 41

Prophet, Nancy Elizabeth (1890 Providence or Orctic Center or Warwick, Rhode Island - 1960 Providence, Rhode Island?) an American woman of color sculptor whose life in Paris and America deserves a full critical biography, 56-58

Purrmann, Hans (1880 Speyer, Germany - 1966 Basel, Switzerland) first studio assistant in the Matisse Académie at 33, boulevard des Invalides, where he also lived from 1908 to 1914; one of the many Germans associated with this school; in 1935 emigrated to Florence, Italy, where he became director of the Villa Romana, a private German institution to support painters, and where he gave haven to non-Jewish artists who couldn't stomach the nazis, until he had to escape in the Swiss consul's motor car to Switzerland in the Autumn of 1943 after the Germans occupied northern Italy (there could be no question of offering refuge to Jews: Purrmann had to meet his good friend from the Paris days, Rudolf Levy, in secret until the Gestapo got its hands on him), 10

Putnam, Samuel (1892 Rossville, Illinois - 1950 Philadelphia, Pennsylvania?) American writer who lived in Paris and wrote about it; founded *The New Review* in 1931; became well-known for his writings on Brazilian literature and culture, 76, 78

Puvis de Chavannes, Pierre (1824 Lyon, France - 1898 Paris) a very famous and successful painter, yes, but to his credit official Salon circles and the successive avant-garde movements' popes never fully accepted him; received a bit of recognition at the end of his life; some of his murals are in the Panthéon, 100

Quarterites fortunate American and British tourists of all genders who lived in or on the borders of the 14th arrondissement at various times, many pretending to be "creative" in some manner, almost all of whom left in 1930, 2

Raspail, Boulevard thoroughfare trod by many an intellectual foot, 8, 21, 35

Rattner, Abraham (1895 Poughkeepsie, New York - 1978 New York City) a far too unknown American painter, 6

Ray, Man (né Emmanuel Radnitsky 1890 Philadelphia, Pennsylvania - 1976 Paris) one of the more incredible American multi-media artists of the century, who lived in Paris, 36-39, 92, 103

Reid Hall a secure (i.e., safe) residence for young American female students in Paris if they belonged to the American Association of University Women, paid their dues and wore white skin; Elizabeth Mills (Mrs. Whitelaw) Reid, the wife of the American Ambassador with private means leased the premises at 4, rue de Chevreuse and loaned the building and the gardens to the Association; still functions as living quarters for young women, although no longer on the basis of skin color, 51, 55

Restaurant Au Moulin Vert a very nice place to eat, especially when the service is careful, 21f.

Rilke, Rainer Maria (1875 - 1926) German lyric symbolist poet and cultural icon of the 20th century who loved Paris even at its most difficult ("Paris is hard. A galley."); served as Rodin's secretary for several years before the 19th century ended in August 1914; loved Balthus' mother and wrote a foreword to the painter's first published work, 36, 40, 84

Roché, Henri Pierre (1879 Paris - 1959 Paris) a great traveller who always came back to Paris; studied at the Académie Julian after which he never stopped painting; author of *Jules et Jim* (1953), *Deux anglaises et le continent* (1956), both of which François Truffaut (1932 Paris - 1984 Paris) made into films, and other books; one of the great donjuans of the 20th century, shared two unique women with the German writer Franz Hessel (1880 Stettin, Germany - 1941 Sanary-sur-mer, France), the Jules to his Jim, 122

Rodin, François Auguste René (1840 Paris - 1917 Meudon, France) sculptor and womanizer for whom the term "male chauvinist pig" was appropriately coined, 8, 31, 33, 54f., 125

Rollins, Theodore Walter "Sonny" (b. 1930 New York City) a colossal saxophone colossus, 18

Romantics the rebellious successors to the Classicists, 28f.

Root, Waverley (1903 Providence, Rhode Island - 1982 Paris) writer of evocative books on food and a longtime resident and lover of Paris; not to be confused with Wambly Bald, who also loved and wrote a great deal about Paris, 14

Rotonde, La café and restaurant from whose terrace one can see Rodin's Balzac if one stretches far enough, 16f., 34, 67, 113

Russell, Morgan (1886 New York City - 1953 near Philadelphia, Pennsylvania) one of the few American painters to use the cubist vocabulary to develop an individual style, 26f.

Sage, Robert (1899 Detroit, Michigan - 1962 Paris) literary journalist and editor who, with his French wife, remained in Brittany in hiding during the German occupation; returned to Paris to continue work for the *New York Herald*, for which he'd worked before the war and when it was called the *Chicago Tribune (Paris Edition)*; about whom more should be known, 13

Saint Gaudens, Augustus (1848 Dublin, Ireland - 1907 Cornish, New Hampshire) formerly popular American sculptor of garden and funerary works, 26, 55, 59

Saint-Pol-Roux-le-Magnifique (né Paul Roux 1861 Saint-Henri,

Bouches-du-Rhône, France - 1940 Brest, France) poet who flamboyantly proselytized a personal school of poetry he called "magnificisme"; threatened to drop from the balcony upon a crowd of non-appreciates during a Symbolist theater "performance" at the Théâtre Moderne on December 11, 1891, when he yelled "If you don't stop laughing, I'll let myself fall on your head!"; honored by a dinner turned into a raucous shindig by André Breton; German soldiers broke into his house in Camaret, Brittany, during the night of 23-24 June 1940, shot the family servant, gravely wounded one of his daughters, and burned the house down, destroying a large number of unpublished manuscripts, shortly after which he died, 25

Sainte-Beuve, Charles-Augustin (1804 Boulogne, France - 1869 Paris) one of the great French literary critics, who lived with his mother; reputed sometime lover of Mrs. Victor Hugo; wrote about their love-affair in the scandalous *Le Livre d'Amour* (1843), 28

Salmon, André (1881 Paris - 1969 Paris) literary journalist and groupie who wrote a great deal about artists and writers he had known, including the painter Henri Hayden, whose life is interesting enough to deserve a full-length biography; one source says this about Salmon: "...began as a cubist disciple of Apollinaire, later joined Dadism [sic], and distinguished himself as a critic of modern painting," none of which is true, but it does give me the opportunity of adding Apollinaire to the index, 107, 122

Salomé a female threat to the stability of certain heads, 42

Sargent, John Singer (1856 Florence, Italy - 1925 London) expatriate American painter of "Madame X" and other daring portraits, 26

Sartre, Jean-Paul (1905 Paris - 1980 Paris) refused the Nobel Prize for Literature, probably while on amphetamines, 18, 63

Satie, Erik [-Alfred Leslie] (1866 Honfleur, France - 1925 Paris) often described as an "unorthodox" composer, whose music, he said, should be as furniture: there but not prominently so, but it is, for which we can be grateful; collaborated with Jean Cocteau and Pablo Picasso on *Parade*, a visually cubist ballet organized by Sergei Diaghilev, a famous impresario of the ballet who is buried on an island in Venice near Ezra Pound and Eager Strivinsky; Satie gave his pieces such names as "Sports et Divertissements," "3 Morceaux," "Jack-in-the-Box," and "Préludes flasques (pour un chien)"; whose composition "Socrate" Roger Shattuck described as an attempt at "a new balance between monotony and variety," which, alas, led him to become the putative father of the minimalist composers of today's ultra boring but lengthy stuff they still insist on calling music, 36, 39, 109, 119

Savage, Augusta Christine (1900 Green Grove Springs, Florida - 1962 Saugerties, New York) American Negro sculptor who gave so much of herself to others that she hardly had anything left for herself; William Rose Benét includes a brief reference to her in his *The Reader's Encyclopedia* (1948), which notes that she is "best known for her studies of Negro heads. One of the four women sculptors commissioned to do work for the World's Fair in New York (1939)," 6, 48ff., 56, 58, 97, 101

Schjerfbeck, Helene (1862 Helsinki - 1946 Saltsjöbaden, Finland) underrated Finnish modernist painter, 5

Schmeling, Max(imilian 1905 Brandenburg, Germany - ?) boxer, 11

Schomberg Center for Research in Black Culture part of the New York Public Library located in Harlem, 46, 48, 56

Scott, William Edouard (1884 Indianapolis, Indiana - 1964?) painter and student of Henry Ossawa Tanner in Paris, 46

Scudder, Janet (1869 Terre Haute, Indiana - 1940 Rockport, Massachusetts) American sculptor of yard kitsch who knew the way to live; bought a house in 1913 in the Paris suburb of Ville d'Avray with a large garden in which to set her as yet unsold pieces; at the onset of the 1939-1945 chapter of The Great 20th Century Aberration she moved back to the USA, 26, 50ff.

Seberg, Jean (1938 Marshalltown, Iowa - 1979 Paris) American actress whose best role was herself in *A bout de souffle* (1960) by Jean-Luc Godard (b. 1930 Paris), in which she played with the formerly ubiquitous Jean-Paul Belmondo (b. 1933 Paris);

she died under mysterious circumstances ruled a suicide by Paris authorities, 63

Seiki, Kuroda Japanese art teacher at the Tokyo Art School's Division of Western Painting; in the 1880s lived in Paris where he studied at the Académie Colarossi, 5

Sélavy, Rrose (? - ?) Marcel Duchamp in drag, 28

Select, Le well-known literary café with excellent ham and cheese fast food, 16

Service, Robert William (1874 Preston, England - 1958 Lancieux, France) English-born North American writer of verse known, no doubt to his chagrin, as the Canadian Kipling, sometime art student, 5

Shakespear, Dorothy (1886 London - 1973 near Cambridge, England) married Ezra Pound in their youth and never found the energy to leave him, except occasionally; her loyalty is admirable; Pound gave her son his name; she made the woodcuts for the long since forgotten work of fiction by the longsince forgotten B. Cyril Windeler (a nom de plume, perhaps?) entitled *Elimus* (Paris: Three Mountains Press, 1923); a lady whose drawings and paintings need to be publicly exhibited, if they can be found, 26, 51

Smith, Albert Alexander (1896 New York City - 1940 Paris) Negro cabaret entertainer and painter, who lived in France from 1928 until his death, 47

Smith, Lynn-Marie the author's muse, *passim*

Soupault, Philippe (1897 Chaville, France - 1990) dadaist then surrealist poet and another Joyce assistant, who abandoned this kind of literature for adventure novels and political analysis, following the money no doubt, for which who can blame him? imprisoned by the nazis, 25

Sperber, Manès (1905 Zablotów, Galicia, Poland - 1989 Paris) writer; premature anti-fascist; leftist refugee from the Gestapo, 28

Sphinx, Le modernist whorehouse in Montparnasse during the 1930s, 75ff.

Stein, Gertrude (1874 Allegheny, Pennsylvania - 1946 Paris) companion of Alice Toklas, 26, 42, 52f., 59, 116, 123, 130

Stein, Leo (1872 Allegheny, Pennsylvania - 1947 Settignano, Italy) Gertrude's brother whose mind may have been finer than his sister's had he been able to focus it on itself as she did hers, 121

Stephens, James (1882 - 1950) an Irish poet of small stature but largish talent whom Joyce picked to finish *Finnegans Wake* if the latter died before the former, one of the latter's curious jokes, one hopes; author of the novel *Crock of Gold* (1912), 40

Sterne, Laurence (1713 - 1768) one of those writers whose lives are sufficiently uncomfortable emotionally, spiritually and economically as to render them devoid of humor, but who somehow possess the wherewithal to invest their writings with lightness and whimsy, touched with acid, it is true, but full of wit and ironic retort, in Sterne's case overlaid with an eccentricity of style and baroque expression dense enough to make the prose difficult to penetrate, but well worth the effort, 88

Strindberg, Johann August (1849 Stockholm - 1912 Stockholm) moody misogynist playwright, who really disliked women, 4

Styron, William Clark (b. 1925 Newport News, Virginia) commonly accepted as one of the leading postwar American novelists, 66ff.

Surrealism a movement, 25, 130

Tanner, Henry Ossawa (1859 Pittsburgh, Pennsylvania - 1937 Paris) American painter longtime resident in France, 41-45, 47, 55f.

Thirion, André one of the culturally-minded young Communist activists who fell deeply under the sway of Surrealism and the debonair Aragon during the late 1920s; one isn't sure whether in the end he was more of one or the other, but he wrote an interesting book about his lives and time called *Révolutionnaires sans révolution* (1972), 35

Three Musketeers of La Coupole, 18

Toklas, Alice Babette (1877 San Francisco - 1967 Paris) longtime resident of Paris, writer, gardener, cook, and the subject of much speculation, 26, 42, 50

transition (1927 Paris - 1938 Paris) avant-garde literary journal, the editors of which did not particularly like Gertrude Stein after she published her memoirs under a curious title, but loved Nora's husband, 13f., 64

Transatlantic Review (1924-1925) short-lived but vital literary journal edited by Ford Madox Ford, but occasionally edited by Ernest Hemingway, which may be the reason for its short life; if you are really interested, see Bernard Poli, *Ford Madox Ford and the* Transatlantic Review (Syracuse University Press, 1967), 64

Treize, Thérèse (née Thérèse Maure 1900 Paris - ?) intimate friend of Kiki's who passed the hat while the rapturous Kiki sang her heart out in the Quarter's clubs and cafés; worked in her own gymnastic studios on the Rue Denfert-Rochereau and elsewhere; changed her family name in order to pursue her life in anonymity (and so as not to embarrass her family); kept a small mouse in a small cage which she carried around the cafés; involved one night in a punch-up outside The Jockey with Pascin who had somehow insulted her; engaged in an erratic love affair with Per Krohg, whose wife Lucy could not break with Pascin until the latter forced the issue by killing himself; in 1930 worked as Alexander Calder's assistant during performances of his wire circus until Calder married Louisa James, a student at Treize's gymnastic studio, who thereafter took over the assistant's position; at Pascin's funeral on June 7, 1930, asked in despair "What's going to happen to all of us now?"; married the Cuban painter Manuel Cano de Castro, 37f.

Triolet, Elsa (1896 Russian Empire - 1970 Paris) wrote her novels and polemics in French, of which a number remained free of marxist-leninist-stalinist cant, 36f.

Trotsky, Léon (né Leib Davydovich Bronstein, (1877 Elisavetgrad, Russia - 1940 Mexico City) failed revolutionary intellectual, 9, 27

Turk, The primitive locus for the evacuation of human waste material, 14

Twydsen, Lady Duff (née Dorothy Smurthwaite, a.k.a. Mary Duff Stirling Byrom Twysden King 1892 Yorkshire, England - 1938 Santa Fe, New Mexico) well-known in the Quarter during her sponge-lush phase when she met Hemingway and the others and appeared in *The Sun Also Rises* (1926), 101

Tzara, Tristan (1896 Moinesti, Romania - 1963, Paris) Moldo-Valachian dadaist, 12, 36

Uhde, Wilhelm (1874 Friedeberg, Germany - 1947 Paris) gay German art dealer and writer; longtime resident of Paris; an early admirer and friend of Picasso whose works he showed in his art gallery called Nôtre-Dame-des-Champs in 1908; the nazis took away his citizenship and he suffered accordingly, living during the war under a false name in the South of France, 10

Underground City, The a novel you should read, 67ff.

Unidentified Flying Idea allegedly a social service organization in Cambridge, Massachusetts, 71

Vassilieff, Marie (née Mariia Ivanova Vasileva 1884 Smolensk, Russia - 1957 Nogent-sur-Marne, France) manager of her own art académie in the Impasse du Maine, in whose sketching class Nina Hamnett would feel compelled to dance a few impromptu steps in the nude; opened her studio in February 1915 as a canteen to provide inexpensive food and drink to penurious artists, the locale of the famous banquet to celebrate the return of the wounded Georges Braque in January 1917, 122

Vavin, Carrefour the geographic social center of the Montparnasse quarter of the city for many non-French inhabitants, 1, 21

Verlaine, Paul (1844 Metz, France - 1896 Paris) about whom one source notes that as a Symbolist poet his work is distinguished for its musical qualities and his life for being disreputable; he did write some beautiful as well as some intensely erotic poems, and he did like his regular snort of absinthe, 132

Vers et Prose (1905 - 1914) literary journal of the then avant-garde edited and published in a herculean effort by Paul Fort; its supporters met regularly at the Closerie des Lilas, 41, 102, 105

Vigny, Alfred de, Comte de (1797 Loches, France - 1863 Paris) successfully played the stoic martyr to his melancholy art; a Romantic poet who retired from the world after an unhappy love affair and for whom the phrase "ivory tower" was coined, 29

Vollmöller, Mathilde (1876 Stuttgart, Germany - 1943 Munich, Germany) painter; student at the Matisse Academy 1909-10, in whose studio at 17, rue Campagne-Première the poet Rilke lived for a few months in 1908 from where he moved into the studio in the Hôtel Biron (77, rue de Varenne) of his sculptor wife who had studied with Rodin, Clara Westhoff-Rilke; married Hans Purrmann in 1912; returned to Germany with her husband after the birth of their second child and after the French confiscated their personal property, 40, 84

Vuillard, Edouard (1867 Cuiseaux, Saône-et-Loire, France - 1940 La Baule, Loire-Inférieure, France) painter of no particular school or talent, whose works are apparently esteemed by curators and other museum employees and bored of directors members, 90

Waring, Laura Wheeler (1887 Hartford, Connecticut - 1948 West Chester, Pennsylvania) American Negro painter who studied in Paris, 7, 47

Washington, Booker Taliaferro (1856 Franklin County, Virginia - 1915 Tuskegee, Alabama) no relation to George or the pop song singer, 42f.

Weisgerber, Albert (1878 St. Ingbert bei Saarbrücken, Germany - 1915 near Fromelles, Ypres, France) German artist; student in Munich; lived in Paris for several years from 1906; his short life ended in the trenchslime of the western front, 10

West, Nathanael (né Nathan Wallenstein Weinstein 1903 New York City - 1940 El Centro, California) American small game hunter and novelist who married someone's sister Eileen, 4

Whistler, James Abbott McNeill (1834 Lowell, Massachusetts - 1903 London) American painter, 26, 28, 40

White, Stanford (1853 New York City - 1906 New York City) architect who designed the Washington Square Arch and loved unwisely, 52

Williams, William Carlos (1883 Rutherford, New Jersey - 1963) one cannot quite decide whether his work lives on because of its originality and independence of "schools" and "theories" or his presence and influence at the right place and time throughout his long and prolific life as both poet and physician; author of the booklength poem *Paterson*, several prose works, hundreds of published poems, an autobiography, a collection of letters, all worth reading despite his often hair-brained and cranky notions and opinions, 37, 116

Woodruff, Hale Aspacio (1900 Cairo, Illinois - 1980 New York City?) American Negro painter who studied in Paris, 47, 101

Wrangel, Count F. U. (1853 - ?) Swedish lord chamberlain to the Swedish queen (until he gambled away her travel allowance at Nice in 1906) and writer of memoirs; settled in Versailles in 1908 where he acted as advisor and father-figure to the young Scandinavian artists who flowed into Paris before 1914; a habitué of the Café de Versailles on the Place du 18 Juin 1940 (formerly Place de Rennes) (6th, 14th and 15th) several blocks west of the Carrefour Vavin; remained in Paris until well into the 1920s with his painter wife, with whom he first lived in Paris 1888-91, 26

Zawadowski, Waclaw (Zawado) Polish painter who arrived in Paris in 1912 and stayed for many years; friend of Kisling and member of the Polish contingent in Montparnasse; moved into Modigliani's studio after the Italian's death in 1920; Nina Hamnett moved in with him in 1921, 108

Zadkine, Ossip (1890 Smolensk, Russia - 1967 Paris) a sculptor who studied with Injalbert at the École des Beaux-Arts, whose museum, where he lived from 1928 until his death (except the period 1941-45 when he lived in exile in New York City), in the 6th arrondissement, is well worth visiting, 63

Zervos, Christian publisher of books of and about modern art, 11

Zola, Émile Edouard Charles Antoine (1840 Paris - 1902 Paris) novelist exemplar of the "naturalism" school of fiction (i.e., "warts and all"), sometimes also referred to as "realism"; debtor and friend of Cézanne's youth, whose remains seem to be both in the Panthéon and the Montmartre Cemetery, 8

Note on the Index

Of a relatively random sample of 172 people mentioned in the Index, of which 25 were born in Paris, 68 died there. (This figure would be higher if the Parisian suburbs, such as Neuilly, were counted as the city, which they aren't). What these figures mean is unclear, but 43 more of these people died in the city than were born there. Which brings to mind the graffito fragment on the rear door of The Edge Bar in Venice, Italy, stumbled upon by Henry James, when, for a brief moment, he lost his way, having been mildly bemused by a tall, if bulky, nordic sailor - a fragment which, when deciphered later by a vacationing Serbo-Croat postal employee, whose English, it must be admitted, did not achieve the heights of lucidity he claimed to have conquered, read "See Paris and die."